Resolving Couples Conflict

A Positive Path to Shared Love, Understanding, Confidence and Hope in Your Relationship

PADDY CYNDY

© Copyright 2023 - All rights reserved.

The content contained within this book may not be reproduced, duplicated or transmitted without direct written permission from the author or the publisher.

Under no circumstances will any blame or legal responsibility be held against the publisher, or author, for any damages, reparation, or monetary loss due to the information contained within this book, either directly or indirectly.

Legal Notice:
This book is copyright protected. It is only for personal use. You cannot amend, distribute, sell, use, quote or paraphrase any part, or the content within this book, without the consent of the author or
publisher.

Disclaimer Notice:
Please note the information contained within this document is for educational and entertainment purposes only. All effort has been executed to present accurate, up to date, reliable, complete information. No warranties of any kind are declared or implied. Readers acknowledge that the author is not engaged in the rendering of legal, financial, medical or professional advice. The content within this book has been derived from various sources. Please consult a licensed professional before attempting any techniques outlined in this book.

By reading this document, the reader agrees that under no circumstances is the author responsible for any losses, direct or indirect, that are incurred as a result of the use of the information contained within this document, including, but not limited to, errors, omissions, or inaccuracies.

Table of Contents

Introduction V

Chapter 1: You Are Both Meant To Be Happy 1

Chapter 2: The Love Must Be Mutual And Actual 17

Chapter 3: Knowing And Meeting Each Other's Needs 33

Chapter 4: Are You Also Friends With Each Other? 43

Chapter 5: Causes Of Conflicts In Relationship 54

Chapter 6: Consequences Of Conflicts On Relationships 66

Chapter 7: Managing And Resolving Conflicts In The
Relationship 71

Chapter 8: The Importance Of Communication In
Marriage 85

Chapter 9: Don't Dissolve It, But Resolve It 100

Chapter 10: There Is Still Hope For Your Future 110

Conclusion 122

References 127

Introduction

So God created man in his own image, in the image of God created him; male and female created him. –King James Bible, 1769/2017, Genesis 1:27

Are you about to enter into marriage, but you are not sure if you are mentally ready? Do you have the skill set to handle conflicts? If you have seen signs of misunderstanding in your relationship before tying the knot, do you know when it is time to quit, or perhaps you think there is hope for the future? Maybe you dread that you are going to lose that relationship, marriage, or ultimately your family through divorce. Are you wondering just how you can prevent this from happening? If this is you, then do not worry, because you are not alone. For example, one 30-year-old woman from Connecticut once told her friend that she feared getting married because the majority of married women she talked to weren't happy, and neither were most of the men too. She then wondered why people even got married in the first place. Everyone she talked to appeared trapped, quitting being themselves, losing their passions, and becoming kind of owned by that other person. Surely at one point in their marriage, people who have been married for a long time, get tired of having sex with the same person, particularly men?

You have probably frequently heard some of the following utterances within your family and community circles: "I regret marrying you!," "I wish I had never met you!," "Oh! Why did I get into this marriage?" With an increasingly depressing global economic outlook, too much financial and social pressure has been brought upon couples. Old or young couples, it just doesn't matter! The truth, however, is that there will always be some form of conflict between couples. Conflict is normal, but your arguments shouldn't turn into personal attacks or efforts to lower the other's self-esteem.

There is no marriage or relationship that has never been subjected to some form of antagonism. By conflict, we specifically mean verbal disagreements and arguments. People disagree sometimes, and that isn't necessarily a bad thing, as you have the right to have a different opinion from your spouse. What's important is that you communicate effectively and in a healthy way that allows you to understand each other better and makes your relationship stronger. Below are some of the common reasons why couples may end up in a conflict:

- Choosing to spend time with others or doing an activity instead of spending time with your spouse or partner.
- Your spouse goes through your phone and disapproves of your texts or calls.
- Your spouse thinks you're cheating or untrustworthy.
- You're avoiding having sex with your spouse.

- Trying to study or work when your spouse needs your attention.

Our lives have become difficult, particularly in the face of the Covid-19 pandemic that has torn families apart due to the negative impact of job losses on the financial well-being of couples. Still, conflict can be constructively used to benefit the couple. Challenge and disagreement within a relationship can encourage growth, deeper understanding, improved communication, and progress toward a goal.

The most critical aspect of conflict that affects the health of a relationship is its resolution. Opinions will always differ, and this is due to the fact that couples do not see everything from the same perspective. To avoid loss of trust and intimacy, or behavior that damages the relationship, the couple will want to ensure that any form of compromise that is needed doesn't leave a bitter taste in any one's mouth. The following steps are important in handling conflict between couples:

- **Eliminate relationship disturbances:** Firstly, it is vital to eliminate the factors that interfere with the process of conflict management. Such factors include feelings of despair, bitterness, and rejection. Failure to remove them prevents both sides in the conflict from listening to each other, thus complicating the situation.

- **Commit to a win-win solution:** Each party must commit to finding a solution that works equally for both. It is not fair for one spouse to win while the other one loses the conflict. Both spouses must be able to reach a compromise that brings motivation and gives them the urge to change their behavior for the improvement of the marriage or relationship.

- **Adopt purposeful listening:** Each spouse must have the skill of listening attentively while the other one is speaking. Both individuals know what a win looks like for them, but now need to purposefully listen to the other, avoiding censorship or judgment. As soon as the spouses have developed a common understanding of the problem, a compromise can be achieved.

- **Brainstorm together as a couple:** Both spouses or partners need to work hand in hand to find the lasting solutions to their conflict. This is only possible if they let go of their egos and start to brainstorm solutions as a team. They need to shed off any suspicions that they might harbor for each other and then work together to reach a compromise that makes their marriage or relationship work.

I am writing this book for the benefit of all couples. There are high levels of conflict and confusion in marriages within our families, societies, and globally, leading to divorce. This is particularly concerning to new couples and as well as the veterans who have been in marriages for years. Drawing from my personal experiences, I am seeking to help couples such as the following:

- Those newly wed couples who are trying to understand how marriage works and how to deal with conflict early in the marriage, before it escalates into something else.

- Couples who have been in a relationship for many years and still have not learned how to handle conflicts in marriage and to keep the love flame burning.

- Couples who are entering into their second or third marriage and willing to make the marriage work.

- Young couples who are planning to get married but are facing financial and other challenges.

Having emigrated to London from Ghana, Africa at the age of 27, I started my family life at a fairly young age. I did my primary and secondary education in Ghana and then undertook my tertiary studies in the United Kingdom. A father of three lovely children, two teenage boys and a preteen girl, I have 12 years experience in full-time church ministry, frequently counseling different couples on marriage and relationships issues. Due to the experience that I gained as the head of my family of five, I am passionate about identifying and managing conflict between couples. I also possess 24 years experience in relationship and over 18 years of marriage to my lovely wife. My objective is to save relationships and mentor couples to rekindle their vows. This passion stems from the staggering statistic of the level of divorce both in the secular and sacred worlds. Helping you gain a better understanding about how to resolve conflicts is deeply important to me because what you're about to learn has also helped my own relationship. In retrospect, I actually wish that my wife and I had known some of the methods of couple conflict resolution before or in the early years of our marriage.

As a couple, whether in a new or old relationship or marriage, you are meant to be happy. You need to learn to trust and respect each other in order to lead a healthy and fulfilling marriage. It is imperative that you recognize the fact that marriage is an institution created by God to be enjoyed and not endured. Everyone should enter into marriage with this positive mindset.

CHAPTER 1

You Are Both Meant to Be Happy

Then our Heavenly Father said, "Man can't live alone; I will create for him an assistant fit to help him."... So the Heavenly Father caused a long sleep to befall the man, and as he was in deep sleep, removed one of his ribs and put flesh in its place; and a woman was made from the rib and God brought her to the man. –King James Bible,
1769/2017, Genesis 2:18–22

When God finished creating the mountains, rivers, and vegetation, he made man. He was glad that he had made a being that would represent him on earth and have dominion over all things. On that sixth day of creation, he also realized that man needed to have a partner who would provide companionship, love, and procreate with him. He decided to take one rib from the man and create a woman. Thus, from that moment, man and woman were joined together and destined to live side by side forever. What he did for man, he did for animals too, as even they were given female partners. As much as we acknowledge the existence of the relationship of couples, we must note that conflict between man and woman is also unavoidable. In most cases, when a couple lives in the same home sharing all expenses as well as the upkeep of the children, there is bound to be huge pressure exerted on the marriage. If not handled correctly, this often results in conflict with devastating consequences for the marriage.

How to Build a Happy Marriage

Weddings bring about dancing, laughter, and lots of fun but beware; being married isn't always a walk in the park. When all the fun and aplomb has come to an end, and the honeymoon is over, reality begins to set in. So much work is required to make the marriage work, and the truth is that it takes a lot to achieve compatibility within the relationship. If you want to live happily ever after, then you need to invest a lot of time and effort into making your marriage successful (Berger, 2019). You might have been married for a long time, or perhaps, you recently said, "I do," but the truth is that you need to understand how you can foster the appropriate environment to enable a happy marriage. Below are some helpful guidelines on how to build a joyful relationship or marriage that I want to share with you. These tips have been gathered over a period of time from my personal experiences with my own marriage as well as that of other couples that I have counseled. Well, here we go!

It Is Acceptable for Couples to Fight

If you take 100 couples and put them in one big hall, then ask those who have never disagreed with their partners to raise their hands, I guess the response will be an overwhelming silence, with no hands being lifted! One of the traits of marriage is conflict because couples can never be happy all the time. Every relationship has its ups and downs, but if they ever engage in a fight, happy couples pay attention to each other's suggestions, no matter how weird they might be (Berger, 2019). That ability to listen to each other's point of view enables the couple to take note of the moments when the argument starts to go off the rails, and then to allow themselves time and space to begin mending the relationship. I have been a marriage counselor for more than a decade and I can attest to the fact that some of the most satisfied couples that I have dealt with have survived some of the most difficult "storms."' So the next time that your spouse disagrees with you, take time to reflect on why they have conflicting ideas to yours. Accept that you are different and it is ok to argue. Each time you are going through a difficult and rocky patch in your marriage, know that it is not the end of the world, and that you are not in an unhappy marriage. What it probably means is that you are in a normal and healthy relationship.

Concentrate on Your Strengths

One of the traits of a good spouse is the ability to focus on the bigger picture and neglect small annoyances. Seeing the bigger picture helps you to only focus on the positives of your relationship. In order to build a happy marriage, you need to acknowledge your spouse's strengths and weaknesses, and establish realistic expectations (Berger, 2019). A good example is that, if you're more knowledgeable in accounting, don't become upset when your spouse fails to stick to the budget. Instead, involve yourself more in planning and shopping for the home provisions or planning for that upcoming vacation. Let your spouse take care of areas that they have the greatest strength in dealing with. For example, if their skill is in cooking, then give them the space and time to prepare meals. Each time you assist your spouse to work on the things that they are strong in, you are enhancing the amount of happiness within your marriage.

Don't Expect Too Much From Your Spouse

An over-dependence on your spouse to complete you sets up your marriage for disaster because such tendencies result in relationships in which you over-rely on your partner for success. The side effect of this type of relationship is that it stunts personal growth. There is also added pressure upon your spouse to perform according to the expectations that you have set. When couples are in a healthy marriage or relationship, they need to avoid going into competition against each other. Instead, they should work together to complement and complete each other (Berger, 2019). By working together, they will have a common cause that can be used to successfully overcome any challenges that can befall their marriage. It is imperative that you cultivate your personal interests and desires, join the class you're keen on, make arrangements with friends, and stop waiting for your partner to fill in the gap. While it's important to not fully depend on your partner in order to maintain a happy marriage, it's also necessary to share common experiences. To be able to motivate our partners to do great things, we need to be creative and implement new activities and interests to strengthen the bond within our relationships. Couples that work together to build unique passions and acquire new skills, such as cooking, or gardening, will be able to evolve together. Happy couples will definitely have a zeal to live a fulfilling life together. Whether it's a passion for travel, a need to start a family together, or a commitment to a general cause, such experiences improve their marriage.

Choose to Love Your Spouse Only

In Song of Solomon 3:4, the Bible says, "I have found the person whom my heart longs for with affection" (*KJB*, 1769/2017). When King Solomon used these words in his psalms, he must have been referring to one of his beloved wives. The truth is that when you find the person that you love, this individual becomes your soul mate. King Solomon teaches us to opt to provide all the love that we have towards our spouses. It is entirely up to you to love your spouse. You are the only one who can determine if your spouse is gorgeous or sexy.. One good way to strengthen attraction for your spouse is by practicing what are known as "attraction thoughts." What you need to do is to concentrate on the personal attributes that make you like your spouse so much. Is it the shape of their legs? Perhaps it's the way they walk, or even their voice! When you love your spouse or partner for who they are, you will enjoy a long and healthy marriage (Berger, 2019).

Always Laugh With Each Other

Life is hard, and every day brings stress, so have the courage to find moments of laughter even during the times when you're struggling. It is the attitude that you display during challenging moments that saves the marriage or relationship. What do I mean here? Well, it is simple enough to understand that if you display a positive attitude in the face of difficult moments, you will also reap positive results, and the opposite is also true. Couples that are humorous have a lot of perspective. It is important for couples to share some good jokes that enable them to laugh in both good and bad times. Laughing is essential for couples because it creates a calm environment that makes them enjoy each other's company. Those texts that appear to be silly but full of humor are good for building and maintaining a good relationship between spouses. Make it a point to watch your best sitcom with your spouse and ensure that you laugh as much as you can during the show. Laughter is the greatest medicine and a great catalyst for establishing long-lasting connections within a marriage.

Be Kind to Each Other

All human beings deserve to be respected and treated with dignity, and so does your spouse or partner. It's imperative that you understand each other and eliminate any negative criticism within your marriage. When you develop a habit of criticizing and judging your spouse, all you are doing is to foster resentment that is counter-productive for the relationship. In terms of the scriptures, under verse 1 Thessalonians 5:11:, the Bible says, "Therefore persuade each other to help each other up, in just the same way as you are doing" (*KJB,* 1769/2017). This verse teaches us that in order to keep everybody happy inside the marriage, both spouses must desist from attacking each other's character when they are upset with each other. Never use words that are derogatory when talking to your spouse. For example, don't call your spouse an idiot! This is demeaning and offensive as it means that you consider them to be stupid. Try and use words that are not provocative in order to build and maintain a happy home.

Appreciate Small Achievements

We need to stand by our spouses during tough times. This is what makes our relationships last longer. If we can walk with our partners during difficult moments, then we should do the same in good times. Our spouses want to see us being supportive during the moments when everything is blissful. Did you know that good things actually occur more frequently than the bad ones, but couples usually fail to utilize those chances to bond with each other? If your spouse tells you something positive next time, for example a promotion in her department at work, pay attention and celebrate with her. Not only are you assisting them to savor the moment, but you are also being grateful for those happy occasions in your marriage.

Be Grateful That You Have Each Other

Familiarity breeds contempt! This is the old adage that describes just how bad it is to get too familiar with someone. It is highly possible to begin taking someone for granted when they are always by your side. What can you do to appreciate the presence of your loved one? The answer is to learn to acknowledge every little thing that they have done. It might be simple things, such as bringing to light something useful that your partner has done, or making them aware of things you admire about them–just do it in an appreciative manner. Everyone needs to feel loved and appreciated, so by being grateful for all the good things that your partner does, not only are you strengthening the relationship, but you are also bringing happiness into your marriage. For instance, if your spouse makes you breakfast in bed on Father's Day or Mother's day, inform them that they have just given you one of the best presents of the year.

Be Receptive to Change

Change is inevitable. Things don't remain the same throughout your life and so does the cycle of relationships. Our relationships, including marriages, are constantly evolving and with these changes come different dynamics that affect us. If you are to lead a happy life in your marriage, then you need to adapt to change and grow as a couple. Things that we valued yesterday will not necessarily be of value in the next few years to come. For instance, last year, a young couple might have considered renting a house in a plush suburb for the sake of fulfilling their egos, but after the birth of their first child, they decide to settle for a modest house in a middle-income suburb, to cut back on costs. It's important to be flexible and understand each one's needs in order to create a balanced and happy marriage until separated by death (Berger, 2019).

Encourage Transparent Communication

Talking to your spouse about everything that concerns your life is one of the best methods of keeping your marriage strong and fruitful. Be transparent about your emotions, always maintaining kindness and respect towards each other when you speak, chat, or send emails. Effective communication is enhanced by a good ability to listen and affording yourself the opportunity to understand the needs of your spouse. Don't develop a habit of only communicating with each other about children and expenses only, but learn to communicate about other social issues that are vital to the existence of your marriage. Your spouse is your best friend, so openly divulge your secrets, thoughts, and feelings to them (University of Rochester Medical Center, 2019).

Make Time for Your Spouse

We live in a complex world that causes us to devote most of our attention to work and household needs. The loser in this "rat race" is the romantic factor. Plans for a romantic evening are usually put on the back burner when one spouse has to complete a work-related project or when the children need to be collected from extra swimming lessons every evening. The honest truth is that you need to allocate time for special romantic dates by either going out or simply staying at home. This is the time when you can send the children away on play dates, or hire a babysitter to watch the children for the evening while you relax, and have a romantic time as a couple. In Ephesians 4:2-3, the Holy Bible says to us, "So, instead of being two, they are now one flesh. Therefore anything God has brought together, no man can separate" (*KJB*, 1769/2017). This verse implies that when a man and woman get married, they become one, and no one can come in between them. This means that there are certain moments when we need to prioritize our marriage and devote less attention to children, work, and friends.

Me-Time Is Important Too

As much as you need to share special moments as a couple, it is important to set aside time for yourself, while also respecting your spouse's need to be alone too. During me-time, we can reflect and recharge our spirits in order to face life's challenges. Time spent alone can also lead to constructive personal thoughts that are viable for the success of the marriage. When we get married and we have children, we often lose that space and freedom that we enjoyed before tying the knot. This is something I am familiar with because it happened to me when I got married. I had to give my wife undivided attention, but I also got some moments alone. So, everything changed with the arrival of our eldest child a few months later because I lost those little precious moments that had been reserved for my personal interests. I now had to help my wife look after the baby, and everyone knows just how much attention is required to raise your first child! Having said this, I advise you to set aside time to go out with friends, enroll at the local gym, or do some voluntary work within your church or community. Do anything that you consider to be constructive and enriching. If you frequently practice this kind of positive behavior, you will find out that the moment you get back home to your wife and children, your energy will be revitalized, making you enjoy being at home. Let me hasten to say that just like men, women can also apply the same tactics mentioned above in order to strengthen their relationships.

Build Trust

Imagine how you would feel if you discovered that your spouse constantly lies to you. This will lead to lack of faith in your spouse, and relationships that are built with lack of trust do not last. In Psalm 85:10, the Bible teaches us that "When affection and faithfulness come together; righteousness and peace kiss each other" (*KJB*, 1769/2017). These wise words from the holy book teach us that love can't be separated from faithfulness. In other words, for love and righteousness to blossom in a relationship, there must be an element of trust between the spouses. Lack of trust can breed negative criticism, malice, defensiveness, and contempt, elements that cause great damage to your marriage. Divorce rates are high amongst couples who constantly engage in activities of a destructive nature, and if you dig deeper, lack of trust is the main cause of these problems.

Forgive and Forget

In Romans 3:10-23, the Bible tells us that, "We are all sinners, all of us are" (*KJB*, 1769/2017). Again, in Romans 3:23-24, we are taught that, "We are all sinners, and do not deserve the kingdom of God" (*KJB*, 1769/2017). No one is perfect, so we must seek God's forgiveness if we intend to be delivered from sin. It is true that someday we will face the Lord in judgment. The Bible teaches us that we must learn to tolerate one another because we are all sinners who make mistakes. Your spouse will at some point hurt your feelings or make you angry, but it's vital to control your emotions, release steam, and carry on with your life. Avoid making reference to the past and ensure that you stay close to your wife or husband in order for you to make the life that you have built for your family succeed. Stand together and ensure that you provide emotional and physical support to each other. Spouses living in a happy marriage are savvy.

They read a lot of material on relationships and also surf the internet for articles on how to strengthen their marriages (University of Rochester Medical Center, 2019). Other happy couples inform you that they have gone through the trials and tribulations of marriage by learning from experience, rather than the old school trial and error type (Temple, 2009). Below are five principles of success that I have acquired by observing the couples that come to me for counseling. I would like to share them with you, with the belief that they will alter the way you handle conflict within your marriage.

- **Being happy is not the most essential requirement of your marriage:** We all want to be joyful, but joy comes and goes. Those couples living within successful marriages will intentionally work on things that bring joy back when life "throws them under the bus."

- **Couples in a viable marriage unearth the value of hanging in:** Particularly when everything gets difficult, they are expected to remain resolute and stand for their spouses. It is important for you to know that time can help couples get over tough moments by exposing them to opportunities that reduce stress and defeat challenges.

- **Don't repeat the same things:** Avoid doing the same things repeatedly because you will achieve the same results. Clever couples have mastered the art of tackling problems by looking at them from different angles in order to obtain new results. Frequently, it's those small changes in approach and behavior that bring the greatest difference in relationships.

- **Your behavior really matters:** Changing habits is important, but you also need to alter your attitudes. Toxic attitudes regularly bring bad vibes and actions.

- **Alter the way you think in order for you to improve your marriage:** What couples think and believe regarding their spouses has an effect on how they look at each other.

Practice Mindfulness

The practice of mindfulness is an ancient tradition that is a key component of the art of meditation. Mindfulness in a marriage encourages positive thinking to avoid thoughts about divorce from the outset (Vincent, 2022). Couples are encouraged to be optimistic and avoid being pessimistic. In Pro 23:7, the Bible tells us that "For as he thinks in his soul, so is he: Eat and imbibe, saith he to thee; But his soul is not with thee." What we can draw from this verse, is that if we think negatively about our marriage or relationship it will break, but positive thinking will cause it to thrive. We need to lift up our hopes and get into the marriage with a full-hearted approach. Let us adopt an attitude that eliminates any reservations and suspicions for one another. Positive thinking must drive our marriages. The following are some of the things that we can implement in your relationship to enhance mindfulness:

- Trust yourself in all the things you engage in.

- Develop new strength and determination.

- Build the strength to achieve your goals.
- Improve all personal and professional associations.
- Get control over your situation.
- Be empathetic to yourself.

When you get married, you don't expect to have conflicts with your spouse. The assumption is that everything will work out smoothly and you will live happily ever after. The reality is that living your life in the company of someone else is quite challenging, particularly if you are inexperienced in relationships. Marriages require effort, dedication, and affection, but they also demand that you respect each other to foster happiness and success (University of Rochester Medical Center, 2019). A marriage centered on affection and respect doesn't just occur. Each spouse has to play their part. When you get involved in a conflict, try not to get angry and don't let yourself become too frustrated. Walk away and calm down if you need to, then discuss the problem again when you're both in a better frame of mind. Compromise on problems so that you both give a little. The following section will test you and your spouse to determine whether you have adequately grasped the concepts of achieving a happy marriage.

Questionnaire and Exercises

Before you proceed to the next chapter, you and your spouse must take time to go through the following relationship-building questions and exercises. Ensure that you diligently respond to the requirements in order for you to show a complete understanding of what we have covered in Chapter 1.

Questionnaire

- What are three qualities you admire about me?
- What's one of your best memories from when we were dating?
- If you could choose the activities that would make a perfect marriage for us, what would they be?
- What do you dislike about your marriage, and what can you do to improve it?
- What are the ten most important things that you would want for your marriage?
- When did you last cry about something, and what was it about?
- If you could wake up tomorrow morning with one new skill or ability, what would you choose?
- What do you like best about our relationship?
- What's something that you'd like to try in our marriage, but you're too scared to try?

- If all of your friends were asked to describe you, which friend's description would be the most accurate and why?

Exercises

Ten Items... Go Exercise

Carry out the following exercise with your spouse. It is known as the Ten Items... Go! Exercise, and it can be undertaken in any place where you and your spouse are alone together. What you need for this simple exercise is just your words and vivid imagination. Decide on a theme, such as "What I appreciate about you," or "The things I want to do for you this month." Then compile a list of ten items that fall within your chosen theme. One partner must lead the exercise and make the first list; alternatively, you may work together, giving each other a chance to list and read out one of the ten things at a time.

CHAPTER 2

The Love Must Be Mutual and Actual

*Whoever does not love does not know God, because God is love. –
King James Bible,
1769/2017, 1 John 4:8*

The foundation of every relationship is love and understanding. The love for each other should not be one-sided but rather mutual. One party should not be trying too hard to please the other spouse, but the effort should be shared and sustained. It must be mutual and actual. True and actual love is sacrificial. 1 John 4:8, encourages us to understand God first, before we can love. God is love and we need his guidance to make our relationships work (*KJB*, 1769/2017). The most significant lesson from this verse is that couples should love each other unconditionally. In order for love to make perfect sense in a marriage, it has to be reciprocal; suffice to say that both spouses must display the same amount of affection for each other. Before we delve deeper into the chapter, we need to look at the definition of love. The Bible teaches us that "God is love. God gave His love to all of us by doing this: He sent His Son unto us that we might follow Him." In 1 John 4:8-10, the Bible also says, "This is the truth about love: not that we loved God, but that He loved us and sent His Son as an atoning sacrifice for our sins." The Bible goes on to teach us that God is love by saying, "If we truly know Him, we ourselves will reflect His love towards others" (KJB, 1769/2017). In 1 John 4:16 the scripture says, "God is love. Whoever survives with love in their heart, lives in God, and God in him" (KJB, 1769/2017). The Merriam Webster dictionary defines love as an attraction based on sexual desire, affection, and tenderness. These feelings must be backed by tenderness and affectionate behavior in order for love to exist.

The Importance of Love in Your Relationship

Love is a seed which needs to be planted, watered, and cultivated for it to grow. In my opinion, this is an apt analogy. We equate love to a seed that has to be placed in compost-fed ground before being watered. After several days, the seed germinates, and a tree or vegetable is produced. If that seed is not properly taken care of, it will rot and die in the soil, and we will not have the wonderful trees and vegetables that we see in our gardens. The same can be said about love! You need to prove the love you have for your spouse or partner through actions and not just words. For instance, buying flowers for your spouse on Valentine's Day or birthday can be one of the best love gestures you can ever show them. Below, we are going to look at some of the pillars of love that are key to the survival of any marriage.

Make Use of the Five Love Languages

You may frequently show affection to the love of your life, but the question is, "Are you ensuring that you have clearly communicated your feelings?" When there is miscommunication in a marriage or relationship, love is usually misinterpreted because the spouses or partners are sending different love signals. The best way to handle your marriage is to make use of the five love languages. These are basically five separate means of giving and receiving love that include: statements of affirmation, quality moments, gift exchanges, gestures of service, and physical touch. We all communicate our feelings of love in different ways, and this means that we also have different expectations when it comes to receiving love. The idea of love languages is the brainchild of Gary Chapman. Based on his experiences in relationship counseling and teaching languages, Chapman developed the five special forms of communicating love (Nguyen, 2020).

The truth is that all of us can relate to the majority of the languages, but then everyone has their own language that speaks to them the most. Finding you and your spouse's basic love language and conversing in that language frequently may lead to a better comprehension of each other's expectations and enable each other's personal growth. Below is an analysis of every one of the five love languages.

- **Statements of affirmation:** People who use words of affirmation to communicate love treasure verbal recognition of affection, in the form of such statements as, "You look sweet today," "I love you," and "I appreciate it when you look at me like that." They also thrive through words of appreciation, verbal recognition, and regular electronic communication, such as chats and any other social media conversations. Their responses to love are triggered by written and verbal actions of affection that make them feel understood and wanted.

- **Quality time:** Individuals who use the love language of quality time are the ones who derive the most satisfaction when their spouse actively indicates the desire to share some of their time with them. When the spouse or partner suggests that they are going to hang-out with them, they don't hesitate to allow them to come through. So, if you're one of these spouses, you will greatly appreciate it when your spouse actively listens to you each time you speak to them. You will also love it when your spouse establishes eye contact with you during your conversations. All you want is to feel the total presence of your spouse as in your opinion; this is the ultimate mark of a successful marriage. Sharing quality time with your better half involves providing unfettered attention to them, without the disturbance of television, social media, or other external interference. My wife is a great example of such a spouse who has a great desire to actively utilize her time with me, engaging in productive discussions and recreational activities.

- **Acts of service:** Spouses who prefer acts of service as a language of love will attach importance to any actions that require their partners to go out of their way to make their life simpler. For such people, it is those small things that matter the most–actions such as giving you warm vegetable soup when you're sick, preparing a hot cup of coffee for you each morning, or collecting your clothes at the dry cleaners for you. This is a love language for all the spouses who believe in sayings such as, "move from words to deeds" or "walk it like you talk it." The people in this category are drawn to those who tell them just how much they appreciate them rather than those who want to spend more time with them. If you want to be adored by the folks in this category of love languages, you need to take care of the minor and major tasks in your marriage or relationship.

- **Gifts:** One of the most popular languages of love is that of gift-giving. This is an age old love language that has resounding effects on improving your marriage. Have you ever noticed just how much the face of your spouse lights up each time you hand over a gift to them? While other spouses consider gifts as just a routine kind gesture of affection from their significant other, others view them as the only yardstick for measuring just how much your spouse loves you. For such people, it is a big deal when they don't receive any presents from their spouses or partners. Their perception of being loved is built upon the amount of gifts that they have received from their spouses. So, when the spouse that values gifts as a token of love is given a present by their lover, they tend to appreciate the symbolic gesture more than the monetary value attached to the present. Spouses with an affinity for this style recognize and treasure the act of giving and receiving presents. They place emphasis on how the gift is selected and handed over to them.

- **Physical touch:** Spouses whose love language is physical touch tend to easily feel loved just by a mere touch, hug, sexual intercourse, or a kiss. If you are in this category, what happens is that when your spouse touches you in an affectionate way, the feeling that you derive from that act might blow your mind. It is a fact that any form of physical intimacy generates fantastic displays of emotion that are affirming and useful in fostering better connections between spouses.

Sustenance and Maintenance of Love

In Ecclesiastes 4:9, the Bible teaches us that, "Two people are stronger than one, because they can work together and become more effective against all adversities" (*KJB*, 1769/2017). The teaching is that, when a couple love each other, they are capable of working together to obtain the best results possible. Thus, if two people are in a marriage or relationship they can easily help each other to meet life's challenges. For instance, when one stumbles along the way and the going gets tough, the other can help them up. The biggest threat to a relationship occurs when someone hits a rough patch, but the other spouse doesn't do anything to help them recover. When it is cold, a couple can get into the same blanket and keep each other warm, but when you are alone, it is impossible to stay warm. We all acknowledge the fact that two people are better prepared to deal with a problem because they can share ideas on how to overcome it. For love to remain strong, it needs to be constantly fed. What are the ways that we can use to sustain or maintain love? Well, below are some of the methods that I recommend for your marriage:

- **Grow the love you have for each other:** The love should be balanced. Sometimes the women will be trying so hard to please the men, but to no avail. And although it happens on both sides, women always bear the brunt of it. 1 Peter 4:8 says, "Above all, have fervent and unfailing love for one another, because love eliminates a lot of sins, it makes you a kind person, and enables you to do good for others" (KJB, 1769/2017). Here, the Bible teaches us that the love for our spouses or partners must never die down. We must continue to cultivate and grow our love for each other in order to make the marriage sustainable. We should use the teachings of the Bible to assist in restoring love, peace, and harmony within our marriages. This is surely one method that a Christian couple can assist each other to shoulder their burdens.

- **Don't stop doing the small things:** It is those small things that matter in life. Desist from overlooking certain actions and dismissing them as useless. Your relationship or marriage is built by a multitude of these small seemingly insignificant actions. So, what you need to know is that the factors that determine the sustainability of love within marriages and relationships hinge upon doing those small things, such as being romantic, embarking on your second honeymoon, undertaking frequent date nights, unplugging from cell phones and laptops, rekindling your vows, and celebrating your successes.

- **Affection:** Affection is that sense of liking, attachment, and care for someone or something (Merriam-Webster, 2022). In 1 Corinthians 7:2, the Bible says, "But due to the temptation to commit infidelity, every man must have a wife and each woman a husband" (*KJB*, 1769/2017). All relationships are built on affection, and what the Bible is teaching us is that we need to have someone to love and hold as a spouse in order to avoid infidelity. Adulterous behavior is prevalent in our communities when couples fail to have affection and respect for each other. Most marriages consist of several forms of affection that include physical touch, sexual intimacy, loving words, and kind gestures. Affection fosters a close bond with your partner. Not all people display affection in similar ways, but spouses usually become familiar with each other's unique methods of fulfilling this need. Those who can't say "I miss you" might display their affection through their behavior, for example. If the amount of affection in your marriage suddenly takes a turn for the worst, you might begin to worry.

- **Acceptance:** Acknowledging that your spouse accepts you for who you are can be conducive to a feeling of belonging in the marriage. Acceptance is not always about you being accepted by your spouse, but it also implies that you feel accepted by your spouse's loved ones as well as being a part of their lives. The feeling of belonging usually increases when your spouse introduces you to family and friends, schedules activities to undertake together, and shares your goals and vision for the future. Where there is a lack of acceptance, there is a general feeling of despondency that makes you feel as if you're occupying the periphery of their life. This definitely isn't a good place to find yourself in. It is important to note that some people are not good at easily opening up, and they could have certain reasons for not exposing you to certain areas of their life. The most devastating thing is that when you are constantly left out of your partner or spouse's life, you fail to see the reason why you need to be in the relationship long term. I recommend that you try inviting your partner or spouse to mix and mingle with your friends and family. Use this opportunity to start a conversation on what it takes to be deemed more significant in their life.

- **Validation:** Not all close partners see things with the same eye, and that's fine. In cases when you don't see eye to eye, you still need to know they've listened to and noted your concerns as well as understanding where you're coming from and where you want to be. It is not uncommon for most couples to find it difficult to function at a similar scale. When your spouse misses your perspective, you tend to feel misunderstood. If they ignore your feelings totally, you might assume that they are ignoring or disrespecting you. If you usually feel validated, but this occurs once or twice, it's probable they experienced an off day. It isn't such a bad idea to hold a conversation to discuss how you feel.

- **Autonomy:** As a relationship grows deeper, partners usually start sharing interests, activities, and other areas of daily life. You start to observe that you're becoming much more of a unit as you get closer and closer to each other. It is imperative to remember that no matter how tight your relationship gets, it's critical to keep your sense of self. While you can possibly have many things in common, it is important to remember that you're two different people with unique ambitions, hobbies, buddies, and principles, and that's not a bad thing. If your identity has begun to get swallowed into theirs, take a moment to reflect on the situation. The mixing of character traits can occur naturally as you get close, but it might also occur when you realize that you need to assume theirs for the relationship to succeed.

- **Security:** A healthy relationship should provide security, but this can be interpreted in several ways. If your relationship is secure, you normally know they respect your boundaries, are comfortable discussing your feelings, and feel physically secure with them. Establishing clear limits can help to enhance your sense of security.

- **Trust:** Trust is often directly related to security. It's difficult to feel safe and secure with a person you don't trust. When you build trust in someone, you are confident that they're going to watch out for you as well as themselves. If you begin to doubt them, try addressing particular behaviors, such as going out late without explanation. This enables you to establish what's going on while discussing communication needs. Trust is something that doesn't happen overnight. It has to be cultivated over time, but can also be lost suddenly. You can repair broken trust, but this needs effort from both spouses with the help of a marriage counselor. Discuss and agree in advance how you'll deal with breaches of trust in the marriage. While your particular response might differ based on the context of a certain situation, you normally have a grand idea about actions you can't tolerate, especially infidelity and lying. Never feel guilty about letting your spouse know those deal breakers.

- **Empathy:** Having empathy implies you can understand how someone else feels. This ability is critical for romantic relationships because it assists people to know each other and strengthen their bonds. For instance, if they don't remember your birthday, you are bound to feel upset and hurt. You fail to imagine just how they could do this to you after ten years together, yet you've never missed their birthday. As soon as you have overcome the initial rush of despair and anger, you begin to think about their side. They've been battling at work of late, and that burnout has begun to affect their sleep. A lot of their mental energy has been consumed by planning the massive all-important project that might turn things around. With all these burdens on their mind, you fathom, it's easy to understand how they completely missed your birthday. You understand that it wasn't intentional on their part, and you obviously know that they regret doing this.

- **Prioritization:** It's pretty usual to want your spouse to make you a priority. You want that reassuring feeling of knowing that you come first, and that as soon as they have fulfilled their own needs, yours will be met next. At times, you also want to make them understand that you need to come first before they even deal with their own needs. That is what love is all about! The reason we are talking about prioritization is that a lot of people have several other important relationships. Occasionally, other people in their life need to be attended to first, as when a friend is facing a huge crisis or a family member is going through an extremely rough patch. It is common, though, for you to feel neglected when you assume that they don't constantly recognize you as a priority in their lives. This makes you wonder why they even waste their time with marriage. In dealing with the issue of prioritization, the best way to handle this is to hold a frank conversation with your spouse. First, tell them why you feel neglected when, let's say, they have not responded to your text messages for more than a day, or they are constantly changing date night to accommodate friends. Then recommend a possible way forward, like responding to chats every evening or calling you to talk instead.

- **Connection:** It's understandable not to undertake all things in your life together. As I have stated earlier on under autonomy, keeping separate interests and associations can be great for personal mental wellness, as well as keeping your relationship healthy. Again, you certainly want to be connected to your spouse, for why would you enter into a marriage if you can't share the things in your life? If there is no connection, you usually feel like an outsider even when you live together. It might appear as if you're different people who are sharing a common living area. This is certainly how you don't want your relationship to proceed. I recommend that you build some connection with your spouse by trying some of the following tricks: seek answers on aspects of their daily life that you probably didn't think about before, then recommend some new activity to do together, seeking to get out of your normal routine by going on a weekend trip together.

- **Space:** Space is equally as important as connection to a relationship. Space inside a relationship or marriage allows you to both have the latitude to undertake your own activities when you need to. You know you are supported, but at the same time you can do your own thing. This practically means that you get to enjoy some privacy. Such privacy can be in the form of separate spaces to work, as well as emotional privacy.

Questionnaire and Exercises

Questionnaire

- Which language of love do you "speak" the most? Give reasons for your response.

- Name five things that you would like your spouse to do to maintain your marriage.

- State five things that you can do to fulfill the needs of your spouse. Give reasons for your answers.

- Name any three occasions you expect your spouse to give you gifts during the year.

- How will you respond to your spouse if they forget to give you a birthday present?

- What are the five things that you love most about your spouse?

- What was the first thing that attracted you to your spouse?

- Over the last five years, what have you done to positively help your marriage or relationship?

Exercises

Acts of Service Challenge

Date Night Challenge: Jacks, Queens, and Kings of Service

What you'll need: Piece of paper, pen, and a pack of playing cards

What to do: On a piece of paper, jot down three "acts of services" that need to be undertaken this coming weekend. They could be household chores, grocery shopping, taking the kids to choir practice–anything that is on your "to do" list. Assign one task to Jacks, one to Queens, and one to Kings. Next, rearrange your pack of cards then put the pile in the center of the table. Give each other chances to draw a card. Each card contains a quick "service" to do for your spouse. Use the list below as a reference. If you pull a Jack, Queen, or King, keep them close to you. The person who collects the most Jacks at the end of each game gets to perform the Jacks act of service that you assigned on your list; the same goes with Queens and Kings. When you both have two Jacks, Queens, or Kings apiece, you must do that activity together!

- Below are some of the things that would typically go on the card that you drew:
- Administer a 20 second shoulder massage to your spouse.
- Offer your spouse a smoothie or a glass of juice.
- Brush your spouse's hair for one minute.

- Inform your spouse about five items they performed this week that you are grateful for.
- Embrace your spouse and kiss them.

On a piece of paper, name one reason why your spouse is fantastic. Fold it up and hand it over to them to open later.

CHAPTER 3

Knowing and Meeting Each Other's Needs

Look not every man on his own things, but every man also on the things of others. –King James Bible,
1769/2017, Philippians 2:3-5

According to Philippians 2:4, the Bible teaches us to take care not only of our own needs but those of others as well. This holds especially true for couples. It is therefore important for you to identify the needs of your spouse and meet them accordingly, as they might differ fundamentally from yours. There are different types of needs, ranging from spiritual to sexual needs, which we will explore in detail below.

Types of Needs

Spiritual needs

Are you suffering from inadequate spiritual intimacy within your marriage or relationship? Perhaps you're not sure? Here are some of the indicators that spiritual intimacy may be lacking in your marriage:

- You constantly fight in many aspects of your marriage.

- You probably feel incapable of leading by example in the eyes of God.

- You don't have boundaries for protecting your marriage.

To meet your spiritual needs as a couple, you both have to submit your lives and commit to a relationship with the Lord. You rise as one spiritually if you follow God's ways and aim to worship Him in everything. Spiritual intimacy is an essential ingredient that enables you to fulfill your spiritual needs. This kind of intimacy is only for those who have an individual relationship with the Heavenly Father through his son, Jesus Christ. When you get married to a Christian, you have a great honor of obtaining spiritual intimacy within your marriage. Each time couples grow in their vertical relationships with God, their horizontal relationship between themselves also benefits quite nicely (Rosberg & Rosberg, 2006).

Spiritual needs must be met through the efforts of both parties to the marriage. It is more rewarding when you experience the greatness of God together and share everything that you've learned. Seek God and avoid making excuses such as, "I am not interested in spiritual things. There are more challenging matters right now." The sad thing is that as a couple, you probably underestimate the power of spiritual intimacy to make your marriage work. You are lured to each other by emotional and physical attractions; however, it is the spiritual bond that binds you together. Below are some of the good things brought by spiritual intimacy in your marriage.

- It permits you to bond successfully.
- It connects you with God.
- It enables you to shower each other with God's love.

I have prepared a list of things that you can do as a couple in order to grow spiritually. You can make use of some of my recommendations that are listed below.

- **Study the Bible:** Set aside daily moments to read God's Word. Always stay in touch with God.
- **Pray together:** No intimacy surpasses joining each other as a couple in prayer.
- **Study together:** Going through Bible studies as a couple can also have profound benefits for your relationship.
- **Teach your children to follow God:** The best thing that you can do as a Christian couple is to pass on your beliefs to your offspring. Work together to make them believe that God is the key to successful living.
- **Count your blessings:** Take time to be grateful to God for all He has given you in life.

Emotional Needs

We all have emotional desires that need to be fulfilled. Think of basic needs such as water, air, food, and shelter. Fulfilling such physical requirements enables you to live, but it requires more to make life meaningful. Things like friendship, love, faith, or gratitude are just as valuable. In a marriage, the strength of your connection can make such a huge difference in determining whether you both get your desires fulfilled or not. The following are characteristics of emotional needs that we need to take note of:

- **Emotional needs aren't cast in stone:** You can have different desires in your life, and these can also change within your marriage. This might occur as you discover more regarding yourself through individual growth or your development as a couple. It's acceptable to change over time, even to unearth needs you never thought of before. Past lessons can have an effect as well.

- **Needs vary from person to person:** Emotional needs are not the same for everyone. Certain people might prefer belonging instead of love, or trust over lust, for instance. While you give priority to particular things, such as bonding, your spouse might value privacy and personal freedom. This is not to say that your marriage has failed, but you might have to put some more effort into discussing ways to meet half-way.

Physical Needs

Tying the knot can be a very satisfying experience, but it is also challenging. Spouses feel appreciated each time their physical requirements in marriage are fulfilled. At times one spouse may require more than the other to experience happiness and contentment. The daily physical requirements in marriage encompass the following: love, sexual satisfaction, recreational friendship, and domestic help. Let's consider some of them in detail below.

- **Attention:** Attention is the need to be recognized and appreciated. It's all about focusing on the needs of your spouse, which may not necessarily be sexual needs. The things that you can do include touching, hugging, massaging and gift-gift-giving. You can also provide attention by exchanging love texts messages, messages and flowers. It is good for couples to give each other presents to commemorate birthdays and special events such as Christmas. The real sad thing is that a couple of years down the line after their marriage, spouses often find themselves in a relationship that is devoid of attention,, and this is not good at all.

- **Domestic support and family commitment:** Domestic support means that spouses must assist with home tasks. Such a commitment can foster a sense of togetherness in the marriage, making daily life more controllable. For women, it goes without saying that they thrive when there is strong family commitment. To a woman, her spouse's eagerness to have children with her implies that he will also be willing to fulfill their children's social and educational growth. Activities that are undertaken here include having dinner as a family and participating in family-oriented sporting events. A lot of spouses should be willing to frequently help around the home more or undertake additional parenting chores to show commitment to family.

- **Quality time and friendship:** Quality time is important to maintaining a sound marriage. By spending quality time with your spouse, you get to understand each other, thereby sharing values and memories. As the saying goes, "those that play together will always stay together." Couples must plan time together to undertake joint activities they both desire (Onu, 2022).

Financial Needs

In Deuteronomy 28:11-12, the Bible says: "And the Lord shall provide plenty of goods, to include the growth of your soul, cattle, and the ground, in the land that the Lord gave your fathers to give you" (*KJB*, 1769/2017).

Through this teaching, we recognize that it is essential to pray for help with fulfilling our financial obligations as couples. God Almighty has the power to provide for our financial needs, and we can only receive his blessings if we pray sincerely. Financial needs are recurring expenditures that will probably consume a significant amount of your paycheck, but that are required for survival. They include mortgage bills, food, electricity, rentals, transportation, insurance, and gas. When these things are not taken care of, the marriage is bound to suffer. As a couple's unpaid bills accumulate, stress builds up, leading to constant unhappiness in the marriage. While we pray to God to help us meet our financial obligations, we must also put in the work to maximize our current income. Our priority should be daily expenses for food, shelter, clothes for the family, and bills. As a couple, you will have to draw up a family budget. Sit down and make a list of your income and your total expenses, and then balance them to see where you stand. If taking care of all your expenses is going to be impossible, you all need to put hands on deck and start cutting back somewhere or seek new or part-time work. Your bills need to be paid off at the agreed times or even quicker if possible.

Sexual Needs

In Genesis 2:24, the Bible tells us that, "Therefore a man will move from his parent's home, and stay close to his wife, and they will become one flesh" (*KJB*, 1769/2017).

This teaching clearly shows us that man and woman should live together to fulfill their sexual needs. Many people are not sure just how much sex should be in their marriages. They are clueless about the amount of sex that will be deemed enough for married couples. Just how essential is sex to the survival of our marriages? Such questions are pretty common and usually asked in most marriage counseling offices.

Sexual satisfaction is an essential physical and emotional requirement. For both men and women, sex is a profound necessity in marriage, but men have greater desires than their counterparts. This is because men have a greater sexual appetite that is fueled by the presence of testosterone in their bodies (Feuerman, 2022). Women must understand that their husbands are easily aroused and visually stimulated by such basic things as the physical appearance of their spouses during intercourse. Women are more different because they need to have feelings for someone first and then respond to being touched in sensitive parts in order to be sexually aroused. Interesting enough, there are different stimulants for sexual activity between men and women. For instance, men participate in sexual activities to fulfill their cravings, while women are generally more concerned about intimacy and emotional bonding. My advice to couples seeking sexual gratification in their relationships is for them to begin exploring everything about each other that turns them on. They will definitely enjoy a more satisfying sex life together. It's also vital to acknowledge the presence of your spouse as intimacy isn't just all about sex. Supporting your spouse each time they need your helping hand is critical for a happy marriage.

Questionnaire and Exercises

Questionnaire

- List five things that make you feel safe and secure in marriage..

- How much do you value sexual satisfaction in our marriage? What can you do to keep the fire burning?

- What are your emotional needs, and how best can they be fulfilled?

- What needs do you want to be fulfilled the most out of this relationship?

- How best do you want to communicate your sexual needs to your spouse?

Exercises

Active Listening Exercise

With your spouse, carry out an undisturbed active listening exercise by basically setting a clock for anywhere between 3 to 5 minutes and then allowing your spouse to speak freely. They can express anything they're thinking about. It can be linked to college, workmates, work issues, the children, marital stress, or anything under the sun. The silent spouse can provide communication assistance through gestures and nonverbal interaction clues, but they can't talk during the allocated time. As soon as time is up, change speakers and carry out the couples' communication exercise again. At the end of the period allocated to each speaker, the silent spouse can inquire to see if they need explanations on any points. This step is necessary as it ensures that everything that was said was comprehended.

CHAPTER 4

Are You Also Friends With Each Other?

A man that hath friends must shew himself friendly: and there is a friend that sticketh closer than a brother. –King James Bible, 1769/2017, Proverbs 18:24

Anyone who has been betrayed by a "lover" on several occasions might be able to understand how bad it feels to have an untrustworthy spouse or partner. This verse teaches us to live with people that you can rely on. If you pray to God to receive a partner who is friendly and reliable, then the Heavenly Father will give you that kind of lover. Proverbs 18:24 (*KJB*, 1769/2017) enlightens us on how we can build long-lasting relationships by being friends first with our partners. Friendships help us to get to know people before we decide to spend the rest of our lives with them. Establishing and growing a friendship before getting into a relationship is ideal for any couple. After attempting to persuade a woman to start a relationship without being friends first, a young man may eventually realize that it is not worth it, and walk away from the girl. The truth about it is that a lot of people have faced this–diving head first into a relationship with someone who doesn't want to be friends first. So, why is it important to establish a friendship prior to dating? Let's go through the reasons below to find our answer.

- **Importance of being friends prior to dating:** It is necessary to build a friendship first before embarking on a romantic relationship. As friends, you will be in a position to first understand the person's character and behavior traits before committing to a long-term relationship. In most cases, diving into relationships without establishing friendship first causes all kinds of problems. There are always unrealistic expectations that are created by this scenario as one party expects more from the other. If you become friends first, it's easy to figure out whether they are the right person to go out with or not.

- **"Dating" other people is possible:** Friendship-first relationships allow a no- strings-attached arrangement that gives you the freedom to see whoever you want to before committing to one person. You're not held down or obliged to see one person. Let's make it clear that you are not sleeping around with anybody, but that you're just befriending people that you might consider having a long-term relationship with in the future. So, the whole point here is that when your future partner wants a friend's first arrangement, go for it, and let them get what they want. You could discover friendship first is a good deal and after all, you might not be interested in being in a relationship with them at a later stage. It's easier to realize that they are not your type while in the friendship stage than when you are emotionally attached to them.

Friendship Is Important for Every Marriage

Proverbs 27:17 says, "Iron improves iron, and one man improves the other" (*KJB*, 1769/2017).

A great friend forces you to get better and makes you accountable. You need to be that type of friend, as well. All friends share the same interests, while best friends can go as far as sharing the good and bad times of life. It goes without saying that your spouse needs to be the best friend that you've ever had in your entire life. Forget the best friends you had in high school and college. Your spouse is the one who will stand by you through thick and thin, so having them as your best friend will be highly beneficial for your marriage. If your spouse is your bestie already, then you should be happy because this makes your relationship work like a well-oiled machine; however, if they aren't, then you need to pay strict attention to this chapter. According to Schnell (2016), "Marriages with happy couples are driven by deep friendship," with the friendship being the vital cog of the engine. Romance and physical gratification can easily be achieved between spouses in a marriage built on friendship.

Friendship is paramount to a joyful and enduring healthy marriage. Studies suggest that spouses with proper friendship are likely to derive greater gratification in their marriage (Schnell, 2016). This is because the bonding between couples is usually five times more significant than the physical attraction. When spouses are friends, they expect to share some quality time together and enjoy each other's company.

Cultivating a friendship when married really requires practice, as well as a lot of time and effort. From experience, I would like to recommend the following marriage friendship-enhancement tactics to assist in keeping the spouses satisfied with each other:

- **Time:** Try and make as much time for each other as possible. Include praying sessions as God always listens to your requests.

- **Communication:** Chat, text, or call one another as often as you can. Never get bored about doing this.

- **Trust:** Transparency and loyalty are the keys to a healthy and lasting relationship.

- **Interests:** Establish and agree on common goals, objectives, and interests. Seek new things to experiment with and conquer while having fun together.

- **Priority:** Ensure that you give top priority to your spouse and make them feel important. Be fair and just to each other while maintaining your closeness. Have empathy and appreciation for your spouse.

A good understanding of your spouse is a crucial step towards fostering and maintaining the friendship between the two of you. Play some games that can expose your knowledge about each other. You can also take a quiz to test each other on the Bible and use this exercise to positively influence your relationship. For example, test yourselves on the Ten Commandments and their implications for your relationship. Ponder questions about Adam and Eve in the Garden of Eden, working as a couple to understand the significance of this story in marriage counseling. Even if physical intimacy dwindles in your marriage, the emotional affection should stay intact. Real friendship is long lasting and prevails over everything.

Be Friends with Your Spouse like Ruth and Naomi

Let's be like Ruth who in the Bible said, "Don't ask me to leave you or to turn away from you. Where you travel I will travel, and where you live I will live. Your family will be my family and your Lord my Lord. Where you demise I will demise, and there I will be laid to rest. May God deal with me, be it harshly, if even death splits us" (*KJB*, 1769/2017, Ruth 1: 16-17). This verse illustrates true friendship and commitment in the relationships between couples. I am fully aware that it has nothing to do with marriage. It is actually about a relationship between a mother-in-law and her daughter-in-law, but I just found the relationship interesting and easily applicable to the relationship between spouses. The big lesson here is that when you make a commitment to your spouse, you are essentially promising them that you will always stand with them and be with them through thick and thin. Just a quick warning though: You should not do this for a toxic spouse. Having said this, I would like to show you five easy methods to turn your friendship into marital bliss.

- **Stay positive:** From the moment you first laid your eyes on your spouse until you came back from your honeymoon, everything regarding your spouse was interesting. You adored their hair, laughed at every little joke they made, and you always enjoyed hearing their voice. In short, everything about them was so fantastic that it made you feel secure with them. The inevitable happens, time passes, and two years down the line, the spark is still there, but not as bright as it used to be during the "honeymoon phase." Slowly, it all starts feeling as if it's a burden to find time for each other. Once such feelings engulf you, you need to realize that this is the time to intentionally begin taking care of your marital friendship, which brings us to the next point.

- **Small gestures matter**: Partners engaged with each other in long-term relationships need to convert the mundane things into better opportunities to relate to each other. Doing some activities together, such as cooking meals, cleaning the garage, or planting vegetables in the backyard garden, can help deepen the connection. Instead of always scrolling through your phones, agree to either split up domestic chores or do them as a team. Use such moments to have meaningful discussions about your day, your goals, or your feelings.

- **Don't fake interest in your spouse:** Are you involved in doing interesting activities as a couple in your spare time? You don't have to share the same likes with your partner or spouse; rather, all you need is the right mindset in order to value and partake in one of the things they are interested in. It is possible that your partner enjoys lawn tennis. Do you really have to become a tennis player overnight in order to be there when they are playing their games? The answer is no! All you need to do is to make an attempt to attend games with them and join in the fun when they win, while sympathizing with them when they lose a game. That's what true friendship is all about!

My Testimony on Marital Friendship

As a minister of the church and an accomplished marriage counselor, I am in daily contact with a lot of couples who are seeking to salvage their ailing marriages or relationships. These are people going through a period of challenges in their romantic lives and genuinely in need of salvation, but what is really lacking in most of these relationships is the friendship factor. So, each time I find my marriage struggling in similar circumstances, I quickly recognize that the biggest problem is the lack of friendship between me and my wife. The fact of the matter is that the longer the time you spend married to one person, the easier it is to begin to lose interest in your spouse. To avoid getting into this sad trap, you simply have to keep igniting the flames of friendship and make sure that the spark of love does not get lost.

Make Your Spouse Your Best Friend

If I ever had any best friend after leaving Ghana, then it can only be one person, and that is without a shadow of doubt, my wife. This is the only person who has faith in my abilities and doesn't second guess my decisions. She will always stick around for me, and her love is unconditional. As a Christian, she notices my flaws, but opts to ignore them while holding my hand and supporting me to be a good church minister. I can't say that we don't experience any pitfalls in our marriage. Certainly, just like any other couple out there, we do have our chunk of challenges, but there are things that I realize have assisted us when seeking to realign our friendship to meet our goals. Below, are some of the methods that we have implemented as a couple in order to help our marriage:

- **Talking everyday:** Each evening after dinner and when the children have gone to bed, we make use of this time to recline on the couch and do nothing but talk. This is the moment we use to discuss everything that will have transpired during the day. While she tells me about the goings on in the hospital ward at her place of work, I tell her about my work, counseling couples. We also take the opportunity to recall and laugh about some of the crazy moments we had in the past eighteen plus years of our marriage. Honestly, who will fail to bond with their spouse if they do what we do? On special days, such as Valentine's Day and our children's birthdays, we talk by candle light in order to take our relationship to the next level and keep it there forever!

- **Being silly also works:** Don't always be serious about everything in your life, because life is too short for this. You are bound to always stress over one thing or another, but try and take it easy. In my relationship, my wife is much more relaxed, while I am usually the nervy one; however, I've noticed that having the ability to control your emotions and goof around a bit usually helps construct a stronger bond. As couples, we all know how laid back we were during the dating phase, playing around and joking freely with each other. This was great fun indeed and brought us closer to each other.

- **Text or chat when at work:** I have met several couples who can't or won't exchange texts or chats during working hours. Why is that? After all, when you were dating, those chats kept coming, no matter how busy you were at work. I remember my wife telling me that she would even go to the bathroom to chat to me, and when I heard this confession, I felt special.

- **Have fun doing something you both like:** In our life, weekly evening prayer meetings are essential and play a pivotal role in fostering our friendship. In the company of other church members, we are able to pray for our marriage and share ideas on how to "keep the fire burning" in the home. The wonderful thing is that by going out to the prayer meetings, we are able to get away from the children, enabling us to freely mix and mingle with other couples. These evening prayers always seem to work some miracle into the friendship with my wife. Really, they do! We are able to openly talk in a great relaxed environment over coffee, tea, and cookies. At a certain point in time, we abandoned the evening prayers, and the results were not encouraging at all. We became more and more distant, a situation that was also worsened by the demands of raising the children. Now, however, aside from attending the evening group prayer meetings, we also take a sabbatical yearly, to commemorate our anniversary. No matter how tight the budget, this is a must, making us realize the importance of our relationship.

- **Pray for one another:** As a man of God, my role is to supplicate for every one of my congregants, including my wife. I made it known to her that I pray for her well-being everyday, and when she told me that she also does the same for me, I was over the moon. We pray for each other, asking God Almighty to bless our jobs, children, marriage, and health in order to strengthen our friendship.

Brothers and sisters in Christ, I would like to remind you that marriage is a difficult assignment because it's a union between two people with flaws, so a lot of effort goes into their friendship. I encourage you to concentrate your efforts on the five steps that I outlined above in order to establish a long-lasting friendship in marriage. After more than 18 years, I still have to remind myself to work on our friendship every day so that it will continue to grow and not get stuck in the mud. I hope that these things will work out for you as well!

Questionnaire and Exercises

Questionnaire

- Write a short paragraph stating what you think I am doing well as a spouse.
- Specify three things that excite you about our relationship.
- Which two things would you like me to change about myself?
- List five exciting things you want me to do for you.
- Name five fears that you have about our relationship.

Exercises

Book Exercise

For the purposes of this exercise, couples must exchange their favorite books, then let each other know what they enjoyed most about it. What effect does the book have on their life? By reading and discussing your spouse's favorite book, you get a good insight into each other's way of thinking, which makes your relationship stronger. This is a good homework exercise, and you can always go through the results together in your next session.

CHAPTER 5

Causes of Conflicts in Relationship

A froward man soweth strife: and a whisperer separateth chief friends. –King James Bible, 1769/2017, Proverbs 16:28

Conflict is an age-old phenomenon that began with Cain and Abel in Genesis 4:5-8, leading to the demise of Abel (*KJB*, 1769/2017). According to Genesis 25:21-26, there was also conflict that took place between Jacob and Esau over their birthright (*KJB*, 1769/2017). Then, according to Genesis 16:1-6, there was conflict between Abraham and Sarah over Hagar and Ishmael (*KJB*, 1769/2017). As tragic as it might be, the case of Cain and Abel gives us an important lesson about living with humility, teaching us how to respect God and ensure that our actions prevent the destructive consequences of our sins. All couples face some kind of conflict in their lives, whether mild or extreme, that impacts their lives. The good news is that conflict is not as bad as we imagine. Each time two healthy and ambitious adults come together in any kind of union, some kind of friction will inevitably occur. They will not see things in the same way, and such differences are unavoidable. When we argue, we always think that our relationships are the worst, but the truth is that we usually don't get the privilege to see things "behind the curtains" for other couples. Everything is a bit hazy, leading you to think other couples never fight or argue over some of the things that rile you and your spouse up. In this chapter, we would like to look at the different kinds of relationship conflicts and how they impact our relationships.

Types of Marital Conflicts

Conflicts of a marital nature can be categorized into two: those that are simple to resolve and the perpetual ones, which cause long-lasting antagonistic relations. The most important thing is to take note of the conflicts and allocate them to the relevant categories. When making the decision to date someone in a long-term relationship, you should anticipate living with some unsolvable issues for the duration of that relationship. All successful marriages consist of conflicts that can be solved and those that are perennial; however, what matters is that these couples have adapted to the perpetual problems. They will never allow these intractable problems to undermine their relationship. Let's look at some general perennial problems that can characterize happy couples' marriages.

- Spouses with varying sexual appetites.
- One spouse is a germaphobe, while the other one is scruffy and can live with all the dirt and clutter in the home.
- Different attitudes towards relatives of either spouse.

Living with a perpetual problem in marriage doesn't necessarily require you to be unhappy about it. You can still maintain a healthy lifestyle if you can use strategies for circumventing the issues relevant to the problem at hand. In rocky marriages, couples usually get stuck in the mud. When such situations occur, they usually get bogged down in the same discussion time and time again, running out of ideas and resolving nothing. The end result is that couples become dejected and, giving in to despair, they seek to end their marriages. Below are some indicators that show that a conflict is gridlocked:

- When you feel your partner is no longer interested in you.
- Continuing to discuss the issue but not taking any steps to solve it.
- Neither spouse is willing to compromise on their position.
- Each time you talk about the subject, you become agitated and hurt.
- Discussions on the matter lack humor and affection.

Solvable matters are usually based on a specific situation, while the habitual problems are ingrained in the marriage and always hinder many conversations (Cearlock, 2021).

Causes of Marital Conflicts

There are several causes that can lead to marital conflict. From financial problems to unfulfilled promises, the list is not small, but the most important thing is how they impact our marriages. Below, let's consider some of these causes in detail.

Financial Stress

Insufficient income is a great contributor to the stress and tension in any marriage, causing a lot of pain and heartache. Most marriages that show great potential can be "brought down to their knees" by problems surrounding finances. If monetary issues become the daily topic in a marriage and are left unchecked, divorce is around the corner! The most common problems occur when spouses don't fully disclose their financial situation to each other, and when one discovers the secret, all hell breaks loose. Being secretive is dangerous to any marriage, and I call it the "master problem." Some of the biggest secrets could be:

- Buying or building a house without informing your spouse.
- Buying a piece of land without telling your spouse.
- Giving out money to family and friends without telling your spouse.

Other problems resulting from financial stress include alimony payments to a spouse from a previous marriage and extravagant purchases of unnecessary things.

Cheating and Falsehoods

Any solid relationship is built on the foundations of fidelity and transparency. The aftermaths of infidelity are demoralizing, hurtful, and demeaning, but it is every spouse's right to establish the reasons why they have been cheated upon. As is well known, infidelity involves a spouse's unfaithful actions, such as engaging in a sexual or romantic affair with someone else. Every case of infidelity is considered differently and satisfies a different desire. The following are some of the types of infidelity:

- **Opportunistic cheating:** This is cheating that happens when the perpetrator is in love and committed to their spouse, but fails to control the temptation to sleep with someone else. Usually, this kind of cheating is compelled by risky chance meetings that involve sex, alcohol, or drug abuse. Not all acts of cheating are premeditated and committed by dissatisfied spouses. In the case of the chance meetings, perhaps the spouse went out clubbing and while drunk became exposed to temptation. As soon as they have committed the act, they begin to feel guilty, but this regret and guilt dissipates as the days go by, without being discovered.

- **Obligatory cheating:** This form of cheating occurs out of fear that avoiding the sexual advances of a person that you know will lead to rejection. You could have a fantastic sexual relationship with your spouse but still cheat on them with someone else because you seek validation. Most cases of obligatory infidelity occur in the workplace, where bosses or team leaders want to have sexual relations with their subordinates in return of favors. This is sexual harassment, and you should report this kind of behavior to any person in a position of authority, including your marriage counselor. It is a fact that some spouses cheat out of duress and feel that there is no other way to avoid being victimized or rejected.

- **Romantic cheating:** This kind of infidelity takes place when the perpetrator has limited emotional connection to their spouse. The spouse could show utmost commitment to their marriage, trying by all means possible to make everything work; however, deep down they are not satisfied romantically. The unsatiated spouse will seek a passionate, romantic connection with someone outside the marriage. It is only their commitment to the marriage and the fear of what people will think that stops them from leaving their spouse. The sad thing is that the spouse who is being cheated on will have to endure the emotional distress from their cheating partner.

- **Conflicted romantic cheating:** In this form of infidelity, the cheater has feelings and sexual appetite for several people at the same time. Despite our expectation of loving one person at a time, it is possible for an individual to be romantically involved with different people simultaneously. Such cases can lead to burnout, stress, and possible depression. This is why these cheating spouses, in their endeavor to avoid inflicting harm on their spouses and romantic partners, frequently end up causing pain to everyone caught in the web of deceit and infidelity.

- **Commemorative cheating:** This kind of infidelity happens when a partner in a committed relationship has no sexual desires for their spouse. It is only the sense of obligation that makes the couple live together. Such types of relationships are caused by great sexual dissatisfaction leading to lack of communication. These people use infidelity as a means of justifying their actions by making themselves believe that they have the obligation to go out of wedlock to satisfy their sexual needs. Some of the things that could be lacking in marriage could be such simple actions as the amount of sex, variety of sexual positions adopted, or freedom to engage in open sexual discussions. Cheaters in this case just want to keep appearances in order to make their marriages last. Most cheaters do not want to carry the "failure" tag, so they will stay in that unsatisfactory marriage while seeking sexual pleasures outside the relationship (Meyer, 2022).

Use of Sex as a Weapon

Couples often inflict vengeance upon each other by using denial of sex as a weapon to settle scores after a fight. Failure to fulfill each other's conjugial rights results in high levels of resentment, tension, and infidelity caused by either spouse, but this is more prevalent in men who engage in extramarital sex to satisfy their testosterone-fuelled sexual desires. Another common tactic of denying sexual pleasure, practiced especially by women, occurs when a spouse wears jeans or pants to sleep. This is a bad tactic because it causes tension within the marriage or relationship.

If denied sex for several years, many Christian men and women are forced to do the unthinkable and sin against God. Even among church leaders, Pastors, ministers and bishops, tactics of sexual rejection can lead to adultery, masturbation, lesbianism, and homosexuality.

Lack of Children

In most cultures, failure to conceive children might not be viewed as a serious threat to a marriage; however, in African and Asian cultures, lack of children in a marriage is a big deal. Lack of children can result in arguments, tension, and cheating perpetrated by both parties, especially men, who engage in adultery just to have children outside the marriage. Infertility results in high stress levels, often negatively impacting the romantic relationship. Below are some of the stresses caused by infertility:

- **Sexual Stress When Attempting to Give Birth:** Your sex life will most likely suffer from the pressures of trying to conceive. Initially, just the discussion of making a baby can be such a huge turn on, but believe me, after a few months of trying, you will not want to hear such a discussion anymore. For couples that are seeking to catch the right fertile moment to conceive, stress can be at an all-time high in their marriage.

- **Fears Your Partner Will Leave:** "I'm scared that my spouse will find another wife who will give him a child." Such types of statements are common and usually uttered by people who fear the end of their marriages due to infertility. Infertility is normally not an issue in strong relationships, and the spouses are able to face reality and talk to each other about their fears. Avoid self-blame and overthinking because this triggers infertility stress.

- **Tension caused by differences in methods of disciplining children:** This is a huge problem when the children involved do not belong to you, but are your spouse's from a previous marriage. When these children come into your space, you might resent them, feel threatened by their presence, and constantly argue with your spouse. The presence of these children can be viewed as overbearing by the other. The presence of children from another marriage can be an even greater problem if they are your own children. Your spouse might not accept these children, which again will cause tension within your marriage.

Interference From In-Laws

If your in-laws frequently turn-up at your house, you are bound to face marital problems. In-laws can be your spouse's parents, brothers, or sisters. Some in-laws are just too nosy and can never give you the time and space to do your own things in your marriage. They normally think that they have the absolute right to give opinions even when not asked to do so, making remarks that are offensive regarding your parenting skills, criticizing your decisions, and gossiping about you. If your spouse can't stand up to these people, the marriage can be doomed even before it takes off. If you are aware that it is completely toxic for your spouse to be surrounded by your in-laws, your first obligation is to your spouse, by setting boundaries that are appropriate (Baumgardner, 2020). In order to manage the influence of your in-laws on your relationship, try the following:

- Limit the amount of time you are in touch with them.
- Plan in advance how you will deal with a visit that you think might go wrong.

- Limit their frequent visits.

Unfulfilled Expectations

Expectations that are unfulfilled and in most cases unreasonable regularly lead to intense antagonism in any marriage. Most spouses commit themselves to a marriage with big dreams and expectations in mind. They envision themselves living a dream life that involves staying in a big mansion, owning a luxurious car, and traveling around the globe to see places of interest. When these figments of their imagination are not met several years into their marriage, it can cause serious relationship rifts when they compare themselves to their peers or relatives who will be enjoying all these benefits. The problem with unmet expectations is that one spouse normally believes that the other is a good mind interpreter and capable of sharing the same expectations; however, agitation sneaks in if things go south. Spouses go for each other's throats as they blame one another for the failure of lifestyle decisions, budgets, in-law expectations, splitting home chores, or even failing to support each other's career preferences.

Bad Company

1 Corinthians 15:33, says, "Don't be misled by people who talk about such things, for evil friends corrupt good people" (*KJB*, 1769/2017).

We need to be careful who we run to for help in times of marital conflict. Some of our so-called friends can destroy our marriages. Some women often advise each other to take charge of the house, but even though a husband can be poor or less educated, he still has his ego as the head of the family. Without being biased, it is acceptable that every institution should always have only one leader at a time. Men must give women respect and dignity within the marriages, but should retain the role of leaders. The people you choose to surround yourself with can greatly influence the success or failure of your marriage or relationship. Bad friends and relatives can corrupt your morals and ethics. When you are facing marital conflict, take time to think about who is advising you in the marriage. Some people are keen on giving bad advice that will further escalate the conflict in your marriage. Bad company can be a trusted friend or family member. Some toxic friends can even end up replacing you in your marriage or relationship by causing your spouse or partner to cheat on you with them.

Questionnaire and Exercises

Questionnaire

- What are the biggest challenges in our marriage?
- Do we want to live together?
- Are the problems that we are facing just temporary or permanent?
- How did our problems begin?
- Do you think we can save our marriage?
- Are you still in love with me, and if so, how can you show it to me?
- Do you have faith in me?

Exercises

Letter Writing Exercise

You and your spouse, or partner are to each write a letter to one another. The letters should convey your desires, fears, and concerns. It is well-known that many people are able to let loose their feelings when given the opportunity to write them down. They prefer this therapeutic exercise to confronting someone directly. Each spouse needs to write a response to the other spouse's letter. You can then share what you have written to each other.

CHAPTER 6

Consequences of Conflicts on Relationships

Wherefore, my beloved brethren, let every man be swift to hear, slow to speak, slow to wrath: For the wrath of man worketh not the righteousness of God. –King James Bible, 1769/2017, James 1:19-20.

Growing up in Africa, I used to listen to my father, who was a Christian, whenever he sat us down around a warm fire every night and gave us advice on many aspects of life, including marriage. I recall one discussion about conflict in marriage, a tension he described as a "cold war" between the spouses. What he was implying was that each time a couple goes into a conflict, the result is a series of negative actions, such as angry outbursts, silent treatment, revenge, and at times rude short answers, particularly by women. In James 1:19-20, the Bible teaches us that we must avoid anger when handling any form of conflict (KJB, 1769/2017). In terms of handling conflict in marriages, what we can learn from this teaching is that we need to pay attention when our spouses speak in order to stop getting upset. Being angry with our spouses is one of the negative consequences of marital conflict that can lead to divorce.

Conflicts can reveal a great deal about the compatibility of a couple. When a spouse starts believing that everything they desire is incompatible with what the other one wants, conflict is inevitable. All conflicts stem from spousal goals that are not aligned to each other. Conflicts in marriages usually result in several physical and psychological problems, including burnout, depression, and other mental disorders. Even though those who are married are normally in better shape than unmarried people, the various conflicts in marriages can result in deteriorating health conditions, on top of heart problems, cancer, and chronic pain. Worse still, marital problems can also affect the children's health, both physical and mental, as well as the spouses' performance and productivity in the workplace.

Effects of Conflict and Stress on Relationships

Conflicts in our relationships are not unusual, and when they do happen, we are left to ponder the correct path to follow. Do we neglect conflict, brush it aside, and move on with our lives? Or should we instead acknowledge that it is there and establish a productive way to deal with it? My role as a marriage counselor is to help you and your spouse find your way through the maze of relationship conflict and its consequences. As we have always said in this book, conflict is unavoidable in any healthy strong relationship. Most couples prefer to have a go at each other time and again, as long as the conflict is minimal, and can be easily resolved. Without conflict and some levels of stress, we might begin to doubt if anyone cares within the marriage. At the same time, conflict has serious, sometimes destructive, consequences on our relationships, as we show in what follows.

Conflict Affects Your Health

Conflict in marriages is a prominent stressor that, if poorly handled, can cause intense emotional distress and despair. Conflict makes spouses live separate lives and hate each other, and in extreme cases, it leads to anxiety, depression, unwarranted anger, and repressive attitudes, especially towards women. By the same token, conflict negatively affects the human body by interfering with the cardiovascular and endocrine functions, as well as with the immune system. Unhealthy marital conflicts can lead to several illnesses and elevate your risks of developing chronic stress disorder. Illnesses such as common flu are generally linked to unresolved conflict (Beaty, 2017).

Physical Pain Resulting From Conflict

Unhealthy conflicts also drive couples to suffer from pain such as migraines, heart aches, as well as pain from sexual and physical abuse. The antagonism between spouses can result in what is scientifically known as the "broken-heart Syndrome." This is a health condition caused by harsh and sudden traumatic experiences. The consequence is extreme pain in the chest that is reminiscent of the way you feel when going through a cardiac arrest. If you have to endure long periods of stress due to conflict in marriage, you could end up reacting to physical touch with extreme caution due to pain.

The Consequences of Marital Conflict on the Children

Children exposed to marital conflict face a higher risk of suffering adjustment issues that include aggressiveness, bad behavior, burnout, and anxiety. We need to understand the impact of conflict on the children, when it comes to their emotions and attitudes, by using two sets of techniques–progressive and regressive–for managing marital conflict (McCoy et al., 2013). Thus, the use of progressive techniques like assistance, affection, and conflict resolution, will induce positive emotional responses, such as happiness from the children. On the flip-side, reliance on regressive tactics such as verbal aggression, physical abuse, and anger trigger negative emotional reactions and attitude problems from children. Regressive marital conflict techniques usually expose children to the risk of developing adjustment issues. Progressive marital antagonism, on the other hand, may serve to arm the children with problem-solving tactics and effective methods of communication, ultimately building better social relations.

Questionnaire and Exercises

Questionnaire

- What are we benefiting from this conflict?
- What can we achieve without conflict?
- What emotions do you go through because of this conflict?
- What can we do to forgive each other?
- Is it possible for us to recognize when the conflict ends? If it's possible, what are the indicators that we can use to recognize the end of our conflict?

Exercises

Trust-Building Exercise

This is a fun activity to try at home as a couple. One spouse must stand behind the other spouse, who will be blindfolded. The next step is for the blindfolded spouse to intentionally fall backward, forcing their spouse to catch them. It seems like a simple game, but it requires trust and belief that the free spouse will indeed catch the blindfolded spouse. The fun part is that instinct might cause the blindfolded spouse to turn around, thinking that their spouse will fail to break their fall. This is indeed a great exercise for fostering teamwork, faith, and feelings of trust and security in the marriage. Please note that this exercise is of a physical nature and requires you to select a safe place to undertake it.

CHAPTER 7

Managing and Resolving Conflicts in the Relationship

Blessed are the peacemakers: for they shall be called the children of God. –King James Bible,
1769/2017, Matthew 5:9

The scripture in the epigraph above is teaching us that when you are in any kind of conflict, you be the first to offer a peaceful resolution. By doing so, you will get rewarded by God. In this chapter we are going to delve into the proper management and resolution of conflicts in relationships. We will consider key strategies that can curb and diffuse conflict. Are you and your husband different from each other? Start looking at those differences from another angle and you will realize that each have a different set of strengths and weaknesses. As husband and wife, you are two unique people who were brought together by God in order to complete each other.

Learn to Tolerate Each Other

The Bible declares in James 5:16 that "Therefore tell your sins to one another and supplicate for each other for you to be healed" (*KJB*, 1769/2017). We are taught that we need to love, forgive, and tolerate one another in order to be delivered from sin. With reference to marriage, couples should learn to work together as a team and avoid antagonism. If they work together, they can function like a double-edged sword that cuts with both sides. Working together in marriage, just like in other aspects of life, enables you to create a strong, united front. Below are two things you can work on to bring tolerance into your marriage.

- **Appreciate the differences between yourselves:** The next time you start hoping that your spouse can be the same as you, think again. Instead, what you should focus on is finding the best way to make your spouse's particular trait work for the benefit of your marriage. Always try to let your spouse know that you appreciate their strengths. By the same token, refrain from using your spouse's differences to find fault with their side of the family. Having a one-sided view of someone can be very dangerous for the survival of your marriage.

- **Thank God for your spouse and their different personality:** It is God's will that brought you and your spouse together in marriage, so He must have had a reason for that, and you should be grateful. Forget about the differences in personality because these are quite insignificant in God's eyes. Just move on with your marriage and make it as strong as you can. Work as a team to be the power-couple that you were created to be.

Six Conflict Resolution Phases of Marriage

In 1Corinthians 1:10, the Bible says to us, "I plead with you, brethren in Jesus name, that you accept each other's thoughts in all you say and avoid divisions among yourselves, but that you be perfectly brought together in mind and thought" (*KJB*, 1769/2017). Most couples want to brush it aside, but, as already shown above, conflict is a common occurrence in all marriages. You can have a fair amount of conflict with pretty bad disagreements, which can't be avoided. Because all marriages have tension, we just have to find a way of dealing with them instead of avoiding them. Conflict can bring couples together or pull them apart, and it is up to us to choose what we want. I believe the former will be the perfect choice.

Below are the six steps for resolving conflicts in a marriage.

Step One

Overcoming conflict requires understanding and acknowledging your differences. When two people come together in a marriage, they bring along different personality traits that can result in conflict. As they say, "opposites attract": one spouse can be a go-getter, while the other one is more relaxed and wants a more structured approach to dealing with situations. Introverts are drawn to extroverts, which may be why they end up married. We embrace variety because it makes life fun and interesting, but after a while, differences can become problematic, if not toxic, as spouses begin to argue over small things, easily overlooking the importance of the other spouse in their lives. I have heard of some petty, yet potentially explosive arguments–for instance, over how to properly fry an egg, or how to keep a budget. In most cases, personalities and backgrounds differ so much that couples might even wonder why God brought them together; however, the only thing to do is to discuss the differences, make adjustments, and then move on. Before you think of divorcing your spouse, take time to think about why God has brought you together. Perhaps there is a reason that you have not yet uncovered, even after twenty years of marriage. I suggest that you keep working on your relationship and try to make things work because you never know when God will change the fortunes of your spouse for the better.

Step Two

In order to get rid of conflict, you need to avoid being selfish. The majority of our differences become bigger the moment we make them feed the greatest source of our problem that is our selfish behavior. Two individuals starting a marriage and attempting to do things selfishly may never experience the togetherness of marriage as ordained by God. Human beings are egotistical in nature, always seeking to be at the top of the food chain, and this unfortunately results in conflict. When you get married, you are handed the chance to get rid of selfishness in your life. The solution for avoiding individualism lies within Jesus Christ our savior, for he demonstrated to us that we must not always seek to be first in everything, but we should also be capable of being last.

Instead of waiting to be served, we should also be prepared to serve others. We must sacrifice for others as much as we would want them to sacrifice themselves for us. We should also learn to love our spouses in just the same way that we love ourselves.

Step Three

Resolving conflict also requires that you show patience and seek peace with your significant other. The Bible, through Romans 12:18, tells us that, "If it can be done, you need to live in peace with all men" (*KJB*, 1769/2017). But is this possible? I have worked with many couples in my life as a marriage coach, but I am yet to see a couple that lives peacefully. Most couples put up appearances and make us believe that their marriage is free of conflict, yet deep down there is so much deceit, infidelity, and fighting. I encourage you to continue to work on your marriage by looking for the best in your spouse. Maintain strong fellowship on a daily basis with your spouse and children. Never give the Devil an opportunity to defeat you by removing you from the people that you love.

Step Four

One of the best ways to resolve conflict is to demonstrate affectionate confrontation. Marriages in which the spouses consider themselves to be good friends, who pay attention to each other's needs, are bound to last till-death-do-them apart! It is imperative that both spouses possess the abilities to be loving and affectionate with each other during confrontation. When you engage your spouse in a tactful and compassionate manner, you are able to resolve your conflict affectionately. Here are some tips we can use to be affectionate in conflict:

- **Consider your motivation:** Be careful that your words do not sting and cause damage. If you raise an issue, will it heal, improve, or destroy your relationship?

- **Watch your attitude:** Learn to talk to your spouse with love and compassion even in times of confrontation. Avoid making unusual and unnecessary demands that are lacking in empathy. Even if you want to be respected, you have to request this in a more loving manner.

- **Consider the circumstances:** Before you open your mouth to start confronting your spouse, consider the environment and timing. It is a wrong idea to confront someone when they are tired after a long day at work. The result will be disastrous. Avoid arguing and criticizing each other in front of the children, relatives, or parents. Again, such occurrences never end well.

- **Consider other facets of your life:** What are the other things that may heap pressure on your marriage? What is the state of mind of your spouse at the moment? Is their mental health good?

- **Ensure that you are not the cause of the problem:** You may begin to accuse your spouse of doing something that you will later realize was caused by you. Make sure that before you open your mouth to verbally attack someone, you have your facts right. Most of the marital conflicts are a direct result of silly things, like false accusations by one spouse to the other.

- **Discuss one thing at a time:** Avoid bringing up several matters at one go, but learn to bring up one topic at a time for discussion. If you unleash a barrage of complaints at one time and think that your spouse will respond kindly, then forget it. The result is just going to be an unpleasant melt-down, leading to a further breakdown in the communication.

- **Seek the facts and avoid judging the intentions of others:** If your spouse forgets to do something important, avoid calling them out and causing unnecessary conflict. Rather, deal with the effects of what needs to be done to rectify the mistake instead of fighting.

- **Hear what your spouse has to say:** Be a good listener and always give others a chance to speak. A spouse who dominates any conversation and doesn't give the other spouse a chance to say anything can break not only the communication flow but ultimately the marriage as well. Try and seek to understand the viewpoints raised by your spouse. Trust me, it is worthwhile!

Step Five

If you want to successfully end your conflict, then you need to seek forgiveness. Relationships built on pleasing each other will not last, no matter how hard you try to make them work. Failure in relationships breeds heartache, and this is the time that you will need to forgive each other in order to deal with hurt. The important factor in keeping a transparent, intimate, and joyful relationship is to forgive each other as quickly as possible. This can only be achieved by building a solid and everlasting relationship with God. In Matthew 6:14–15, we are taught that we must learn to forgive each other in order for God to also forgive us (*KJB*, 1769/2017). In this verse, Jesus said, "If you forgive other people for their mistakes, your God will also have mercy upon you, but if you fail to forgive others, then God will be harsh with your misdemeanors" (*KJB*, 1769/2017). To forgive is to stop being resentful, to resist the temptation to punish, and to willingly let your spouse off the hook. Forgiveness must not be proffered under conditions of duress, making your spouse feel bad in the process; the process must happen in love and tenderness.

Step Six

Conflict resolution demands giving a blessing in incidents where you have been insulted. In the words of 1Peter 3:8-9, "To conclude, you all need to have sympathy and humbleness and avoid responding with evil for evil, rather give back a blessing; because you were called to inherit a blessing" (*KJB*, 1769/2017). In marriages, it is either the "Offense-for-Offense" or the "Blessing-for-Offense" relationship. Spouses become "skilled" at exchanging offensive words with each other over the way they dress, cook, talk, or eat. A lot of couples simply don't have a clue how to talk to each other. How do you give back a blessing for an insult and fulfill the word of the Heavenly Father? The answer lies in the words of 1Peter in verses 10-11, when he says "For those who need life, to love and live the good days, they must protect their tongue from speaking evil and their lips from saying deceit. They must move away from evil and start to do good; they must look for peace and live it" (KJB, 1769/2017). When your spouse insults you, you must not retaliate with angry words, but instead you must seek to step aside, allow your spouses to cool off, and then give them the blessing. For you to achieve this, you need God's help and the work of the Holy Spirit. In addition to seeking Divine intervention, you too must display kindness by speaking softly and touching your spouse gently to make them feel special.

Seven Commandments for Solving Low-Level Conflict

Recall the distinction we made in an earlier chapter between perpetual conflicts and those that can be resolved. In what follows, let's look at some of the ways that can help us deal with low conflict situations as quickly as possible whenever we are angry:

- Always sleep in your marital bedroom.
- Never go to sleep in the living room.
- Avoid sleeping at a friend's house.
- Avoid taking refuge in a family member's house.
- Don't go and sleep in a hotel.
- Avoid sleeping on the floor in the same room occupied by your spouse.

- Always sleep under the same blankets even if you don't face each other. (It is a positive start)

Learn to Compromise

- In Romans 12:18, we learn that we must compromise and live in peace with everyone, including our spouses and children. The verse says, "If possible, as much as you can try, live in peace with all those around you" (*KJB*, 1769/2017). No matter how healthy and joyful your relationship is, the fact still remains that you are different from your spouse. As stated earlier, there will always be differences of opinion that result in disagreements. Perhaps you like to eat healthy vegan meals each time you go out on date night, yet your spouse prefers to binge on junk greasy meals. Maybe you like to watch the English Premier League soccer matches on cable TV every Saturday, but your spouse prefers watching ice hockey instead; whatever you prefer, you just have to strike a compromise in order to make the marriage work. Your perspectives may differ significantly. But you have to strike that balance that promotes peace and prosperity in your home. Every day, we have to make a compromise of some sort in order to accept the needs of our spouses or partners. This is what prevents our relationships from becoming toxic. Compromise isn't necessarily surrendering your rights, freedom, or dignity, but it simply means that you try to see things in the same way as your spouse does in order to avoid conflict. The good thing is that you still keep your personal beliefs and preferences, while at the same time reaching an agreement with your spouse and keeping your marriage healthy. Not all of us are privileged to have been taught how to compromise in our relationships, so others might find it difficult to meet someone in the middle. Below are some of the practices that you can adopt to practice non-toxic compromising in your marriages:

- **Sacrifice is mutual:** Because we are all different, it goes without saying that in a lot of marriages, one spouse might be willing to sacrifice more than the other in order to reach a compromise. Some people are by nature good and want to avoid antagonism in their lives, so they will be the first to yield to the pressure of an argument and opt to compromise just to make the other person happy. While on the surface this practice might look good, and such people can be commended for their sacrifice, in reality, it is not acceptable. This is a typical characteristic of a toxic marriage in which one spouse deems himself or herself superior to the other. I can say that this is more common in narcissistic relationships in which one spouse is more demanding and domineering than the other. Such a scenario creates resentment, agitation, and sadness because the other spouse feels disenfranchised in the ownership of the relationship. The bottom line is that no one's perspective is better than the other's, and therefore it is everyone's obligation to compromise to save the marriage.

- **Intentions must be good:** For your marriage to survive, your intention must be to love your significant other even if you are not always comfortable with the way they treat you. You will make an attempt to sacrifice for the sake of the relationship. This is what is important to you, so you will do your best to get to that point of agreement. In any strong marriage, both spouses are keen to see the improvement of their relationship, so they will reach a compromise using a peaceful approach and humble attitude to settle the problem at hand (Adcock, 2021).

- **Keep your unique identities:** It is critical for spouses to honor their values and principles and avoid fully letting go of those things that define who they are, even though the aim of compromising is to work as a team to maintain a healthy marriage. The moment you forfeit your identity, you also give up originality, thus making you fail to make your presence felt in the marriage (Adcock, 2021).

- **Communication is a tool of compromise:** Compromising is similar to negotiation. Both require strong communication skills. When one person feels like giving up, compromise becomes unlikely, if not impossible. However, when spouses communicate openly, neither one will feel they are being taken advantage of, and a solution will emerge that will leave little space for hatred or resentment in the relationship.

- **Use sex as a productive tool:** In Chapter 5, we highlighted the extent to which the denial of sex can be used as a weapon to settle relationship differences. This is absolutely unchristian and unhealthy for any marriage. Sex must be used rather as a productive tool because it is a pleasurable gift that should be enjoyed by both spouses, and not a weapon to make one person submit to the other's demands. Couples can actually learn to productively use sex to settle their conflicts quickly.

It is not simple to compromise because none of us are born to do it well, but we need to be patient with our spouses or partners when we seek to establish common ground in our relationships. While certain compromises are challenging to the marriage, others may feel simple to attain. All you need is to remain focused and be as consistent as you can in order to reach your goals. As soon as you establish the art of compromising in your relationship, you will begin to reap the rewards. In the long-term, the use of the word "compromise" will not cause any panic in your life because you will have the knowledge of how to apply the process to benefit your marriage (Adcock, 2021).

Questionnaire and Exercises

Questionnaire

- When can we trust each other?
- What can I do to make you trust me?
- How can we make trust help us deal with conflict?
- What does the word "trust" mean to you?
- What things can we put in place to build trust among us?

Exercises

Feel-Good Exercise

For this exercise, avoid disturbances from television, radio, and computers for at least ten minutes per day. Take time to talk to each other within these ten minutes, sharing the things you are grateful about. Do not disturb each other. This exercise breeds positive thinking and enhances self-confidence.

CHAPTER 8

The Importance of Communication in Marriage

Let your speech be always with grace, seasoned with salt, that ye may know how ye ought to answer every man. –King James Bible, 1769/2017, Colossians 4:6

So, in Colossians 4:2-6, Paul gives us three significant teachings. Firstly, he tells us to converse with the Lord prior to talking to other people (*KJB*, 1769/2017). Secondly, he advises us to tell other people the things that we would also appreciate hearing and doing (*KJB*, 1769/2017). Thirdly, he tells us to share the gospel before we close our mouths (*KJB*, 1769/2017). In the marital context, what this implies is that we should realize the importance of good communication with our spouses. Communication makes us understand one another and helps us reduce the amount of conflict in our marriages. Communication can be verbal or written, and if you are not confident in speaking out your mind, you can express yourself in writing. This chapter emphasizes the importance of communication in relationships and explores how we can use it to improve our marriages.

Marriage Communication Styles

It takes a lot of effort and commitment to build a healthy and strong relationship or marriage. A lot of couples have struggled to keep their marriages intact lately due to the COVID pandemic. Many things have changed due to the social pressures and financial challenges brought about by this virus. Couples have had to spend a lot of time together, away from friends and even family members, and to manage business and home life in a new way. In the face of these developments, communication has become paramount to the survival of our marriages. There are several things that we can do as a couple to strengthen communication in our relationships. The initial step is to know and foster an understanding of the several styles of communication, which are as follows:

- **Passive communication:** People with a passive communication style often try to avoid letting their emotions, opinions, and desires be known (Bonnie, 2020). They are unable to assert themselves and incapable of establishing proper boundaries to govern their marriages or relationships. It is common for spouses exhibiting this kind of communication style to bottle up things inside until they can't hold them anymore, resulting in a dangerous "explosion." As soon as the confrontation is over, the passive communicator is usually overcome by a sense of guilt. They become apologetic and as usual, will go back to the habit of keeping their problems to themselves, not sharing them with their spouse.

- **Aggressive communication:** Spouses or partners with an aggressive communication style usually speak loudly, regularly interrupt the other spouse when they are talking, criticize everyone, blame and embarrass their spouse, and dominate or control their spouse (Bonnie, 2020). People with an aggressive communication style tend to possess a narcissistic personality, often putting their personal needs ahead of their spouse's.

- **Passive-aggressive communication:** People who display a passive-aggressive style of communication try to alert their spouses about their needs using indirect methods. They normally appear passive, but the truth is that they are highly concerned about their personal needs. Such people regularly feel powerless and show their agitation in more subtle ways, such as the rolling of eyes, making sarcastic remarks, murmuring to themselves in dissatisfaction, or even going to the extent of refusing to acknowledge that they are facing a crisis (Bonnie, 2020).

- **Assertive communication style:** Spouses displaying an assertive communication style are clear about what they want from their relationship. These individuals are capable of advocating, identifying, and expressing their emotions and needs without disregarding the feelings of their spouses or partners. They are not selfish and tend to value the needs of their spouses in the same manner that they treasure their own needs and feelings. When they speak, they do so in a cool, respectful, and precise tone. Assertive people are also good listeners who allow their spouses to speak without interrupting them. Another characteristic of assertive individuals is that they value the boundaries set by their spouses, while at the same time expecting their own limits to be acknowledged and respected as well. Assertive spouses also have a lot of self-control and can easily build connections with their spouses as well as other people outside their marriage, such as in-laws, friends, and the community (Bonnie, 2020).

It is important to note that the style of communication we use is motivated by the relationships we establish, the manner in which we communicate with our spouses, our experiences, our culture, and several other factors. Having a spouse who has a different communication style from yours is neither uncommon nor bad. In most cases, a combination of communication styles usually results in toxic relationships. For instance, a relationship that brings a passive and an aggressive personality together will mean that the obligations of the passive spouse or partner will hardly be fulfilled. A happy and strong marriage enables the demands of both spouses to be communicated, respected, and fulfilled.

Types of Marriage Communication

Communication plays a pivotal role in any successful marriage. Spouses in healthy marriages are generally satisfied and engage each other using positive conversations. In contrast, bad communication is one of the main reasons why marriages fail. As we have stated before, communication defines the state of health of any marriage or relationship. Spouses who nag and complain are not practicing effective communication within their marriages. Below, we look at some of the types of communication, and how our relationships can benefit from them. Please note that these communication styles are interlinked.

- **Emotional:** Emotional communication is important when we express ourselves. How we respond to any situation explains a lot about our thoughts and emotions. Our reactions also affect the manner in which other people, especially our spouses, communicate and relate to us (Rush, 2020). When your spouse gets upset and you display sorrow, they will understand that you are empathizing with them. The result is a stronger bond that fosters better relations and discussions.

- **Nonverbal:** The use of nonverbal communication allows us to display our ideas and emotions without opening our mouths to speak. We can communicate with our spouses through the use of gestures, body language, as well as facial expressions. Our spouses depend on visible communication to understand all these cues. We can never underestimate the importance of nonverbal communication in our marriages. Each time your spouse grins or frowns, you automatically reach a conclusion regarding the thoughts running through their mind on the topic under discussion (Rush, 2020). When your spouse rolls their eyes or interjects when you are in midconversation, you probably will be upset. This is the reason why actions are said to "speak louder than words."

- **Verbal:** Verbal communication is not simply the use of words and phrases, but also the use of language that our spouses understand (Rush, 2020). It is therefore important that we know how to construct and speak coherent sentences without showing any tendencies to go off-topic. When you talk, ensure that your spouse follows the conversation and frequently ask questions to confirm their understanding of the topic.

- **Visual:** Visual communication makes use of your sight. When you show interest in anything, you show it by looking at it with intention. The manner in which you look at your spouse can make them see the amount of affection you have for them. When someone is attractive to you, you use your eyes to inspect their appearance (Rush, 2020). In this case, your spouse will also establish eye contact in return. They will also make use of nonverbal signs, such as a smile, to show you how they feel.

The Role of Communication in Marriage

A good point to begin with is to have thorough knowledge of the essence of communication. Below, let's now look at some of the important roles communication can play in our relationships:

- **It enhances respect:** Good and sound conversations within a marriage enhance both spouses' abilities to respect one another. Each time you need to say something, whether right or wrong, go ahead and say it. Your spouse might have an understanding of a situation that you aren't anticipating, and working together as a team to deal with it might assist in strengthening your bond. When you trust your spouse to help you handle a situation, you are sending a strong message that you respect them well enough to take care of things that affect your well-being.

- **It eliminates guesswork:** Honesty is one of the building blocks of a strong marriage. A healthy relationship with someone is based on transparency, not a series of lies. When you tell the truth, you reduce the amount of stress in your life, thus making your marriage easier and your life happier.

- **It assists in preventing chaos:** As much as we can grow closer to our spouses and partners, all marriages consist of two unique people. We need to acknowledge that everyone has bad moments that can be worsened by miscommunication. Hence the importance of practicing effective communication techniques in your marriage. Each time we are able to clearly express ourselves to our spouses, covering all areas that need to be addressed; it becomes easier to be understood by them. The great thing is that the people we love also come to believe that every time we speak, it is only the truth that will come out of our mouths. This results in a much stronger type of marriage, eliminating the pressure that you face when you are worried about doing or saying something wrong.

- **It fosters trust:** Trust is a key factor in any relationship, but it needs to be earned. There is an investment of time and effort that is required to build trust. The relationship thrives on trust, and without this crucial factor, it will not survive. Lack of trust contributes immensely to the collapse of a marriage in the long term. Therefore, both spouses need to be open with each other, communicating in good faith so as to make their marriage more secure.

- **It brings spouses together:** It is difficult to bond within a marriage that lacks good communication techniques between the spouses. When faced by a crisis, such as a financial melt-down, couples with undefined communication channels can end up fighting on a daily basis. We need to rely on our spouses for support in any situation, and this can only be possible if we are good communicators. Good spouses are reliable and always gladly offer a helping hand to save their partner in a crisis. You need to remember that nothing can improve if your partner doesn't have a clue that anything is bad. If you can work on strengthening your communication skills, you'll be better able to meet each other's needs.

People usually acknowledge that communication is important to the well-being of any healthy marriage. This is because so many things depend on your ability to convey your message to each other. Communication affects your attitude, your affection for one another, as well as the daily stress levels. In Matthew 18:15 we are told that "If your brother or sister do wrong in the eyes of God, go and show them their error, away from everyone. If they hear you, you have convinced them" (*KJB*, 1769/2017).This verse is teaching us just how important it is to be able to communicate with a spouse in order to reach out and correct their wrongdoing. You need to be tactful when you rebuke a spouse as you don't want them to feel embarrassed. If you're in public, take them aside, away from others, and show them the right way to deal with a situation.

What Does Great Marriage Communication Look Like?

Communication in marriages and relationships can be compared to the movements of a river. Whenever thoughts and feelings flow smoothly between spouses or partners, it feels fantastic, whereas tensions cause turbulent communication, when everything becomes engulfed in danger and destruction. Whenever communication becomes restricted, the amount of pressure also increases, and each time the words begin moving again, they tend to suddenly burst in a devastating flood.

Since a lot of married people struggle with establishing and managing healthy communication, particularly when it involves critical issues, it's common for couples to sidestep dealing with challenging conversations. Instead, they exchange more or less trivial bits of information about various activities, such as picking up the children from school or taking the dog to the vet. In the meantime, they avoid critical conversations relevant to the survival of their marriage. The result of a disrupted communication flow is that over a period of time, the love between the spouses dies down.

Having established the importance of a communication flow, let's consider now what effective marriage communication entails. In a successful relationship or marriage, couples talk to each other freely and frankly about highly private matters. They are comfortable and usually express their concerns and emotions in the face of challenges, or discuss their positive ideas when things are working out for them. Both spouses speak in a tactful manner, exercising caution to avoid use of aggressive, painful, or damaging comments. They listen and pay close attention in a bid to understand their spouse's perspective. Thus, they show empathy and eschew judgments. When the conversation is over, both spouses feel great about their constructive discussion while wishing that they can always treat each other with such respect when communicating. The spouses are aware of the fact that if their daily communication is effective, the chances of addressing their concerns will be much higher. In such circumstances, the spouses always eagerly look forward to the chance of meeting each other again, whether to address minor issues or confront challenging matters.

Improving Communication in Marriage

In Ephesians 5:25, we are taught that "Husbands, learn to love the wives that God gave you, in the same manner as Christ loved the church, and sacrificed himself for it" (*KJB*, 1769/2017). By loving your spouse, you will also become a good communicator. In order to understand communication in marriage, let's start by considering the basic biological difference between girls' and boys' brains. When boys are still at the fetus phase of development in the womb, their brains become covered in testosterone. Testosterone breaks neurological transmission occurring between the left and right brain spheres. These are the connections that link emotion to communication. Girls have brains with a lot of estrogen, and this gives their brains the ability to keep the interconnection between emotions and communication. This explains why the majority of women are great communicators, whereas most men struggle to communicate what is on their minds. Now we can see why communication in marriage between spouses is difficult. For your marriage to be fantastic, you must be a super communicator with your spouse. Let's go then over some ways that we can use to improve communication in our marriage:

- **Learn to listen:** Listening is an art. Some people are poor listeners, always missing the point because they don't pay attention when someone is talking. In marriages, we often find that each time emotions run wild, each spouse insists on getting their point heard. When this happens, a power struggle erupts, causing the spouses to possibly lose interest in the conversation and finding a resolution. To avoid such occurrences, avoid interrupting each other when you talk. It is only fair to let one spouse speak while the other one listens attentively. When you constantly interrupt someone when they are speaking, it gives the impression that whatever they are saying is not relevant. The reason you enter a conversation should be to listen and hear each other out, so desist from interrupting your spouse when they talk.

  It is against this background that the Apostle James declares in James 1:19-20 that "Wherefore, my beloved brethren, let every man be swift to hear, slow to speak, slow to wrath: For the wrath of man worketh not the righteousness of God" (KJB, 1769/2017). This scripture teaches us that, God gave us two ears and one mouth for a reason, to have a very good listening ability and take our time to respond to issues when we have to talk to our spouses.

- **Be caring:** When talking to your spouse, try to remember that it's important to show a lot of compassion because communication strengthens the relationship bond. You need to get into the shoes of your spouse and try to understand why they are feeling like they do. Are they prepared to give you all the facts, or do they just want to draw your attention? Regardless, do not discount their feelings and give them the respect that they deserve. Show empathy, instead of criticizing them, and your spouse will love and respect you more because it is the small things that matter.

- **Avoid profanity:** Always mind your words because effective communication can be destroyed by uttering obscene language and name calling. It is also dangerous to always refer to things that happened in the past and use them to blame your spouse. Desist from constantly using the words "you" or "you always" in your conversations. Such words bring negativity into your relationship. You must attempt to use your spouse's name in a loving and caring manner instead of a derogatory way. I love this tactic because it neutralizes anger, while altering the mood of the conversation.

- **Know your facts:** A law that governs communication between older spouses states, "If you don't have proof, then don't ask about it." You must make sure that before you can approach your spouse with any accusations, you need to demonstrate the proof first. A lot of spouses have cheated on their significant other simply because they were always accused of cheating. While petty jealousy is possible in a marriage, issues surrounding love must be treated with caution as you need to be thorough with your investigations before accusing anyone.

- **Be civil:** For a marital conversation to be effective, you both need to avoid giving each other the cold shoulder. The silent treatment will not work if you want to improve your marital relationship. Always try to have a candid and constructive dialogue. If your spouse is addressing you, answer calmly and clearly, leaving no room for gray areas. If your spouse wants to talk, but finds you busy, schedule a time when it is convenient for both of you. Never walk out and slam the door behind a spouse who is willing to talk to you. It is within your best interest to talk to each other and deal with the conflict in a mature manner.

- **Pay attention to body language:** A great way to communicate with your partner or spouse is by simply observing their body movement. Body language can speak volumes about your spouse's mood. You are the one who knows your partner the best and can therefore interpret their body language, so use it to your advantage during communication. Some spouses are particularly effective at using body language to convey their feelings during conversations. Each time your spouse speaks, pay attention to their body movement and learn to interpret it. For instance, leaning forward implies that a spouse is interested in what you are telling them, while shifting eye contact suggests dishonesty. Understand your spouse's body language because it can help you determine if you see eye to eye in a conflict or not.

To sum up this chapter, powerful communication is a key component of any marriage. Whether verbal or nonverbal, spoken or written, communication is a vital interpersonal skill that both spouses must possess and practice in order to improve their relationship. Some effective communication tactics for married people include listening, fighting fair, working with facts, showing respect and affection, being sincere, paying attention, and avoiding use of vulgar language. I also recommend watching videos on marital relations as well as taking part in church-based marriage guidance programs in order to learn more about conflict resolution.

Communication suffers when spouses become too busy juggling several responsibilities as well as getting so caught up in the daily grind that they eventually lose their bond. Communication and transparency also enhance intimacy between spouses or partners. We all want our marriages to be filled with romantic moments and memories in order for us to remain loyal to our spouses. To that end, we need to allocate time to share intimate details with our spouses as this is the only way to build effective communication in the marriage.

Questionnaire and Exercises

Questionnaire

- Why is it important for us to communicate in our marriage?
- Why are discussions in our marriage difficult?
- How can we improve our marital communication?

Exercises

Couple's Exercise

The following is a "couple's exercise" that you must undertake in front of each other weekly. In this exercise both of you will speak honestly, with empathy about your marriage for an hour. Next, spouses can openly discuss ways to improve their relationship and find ways to resolve the things that are not working out. The listening spouse must not be judgemental and should avoid overreacting. This trust-building exercise will help partners or spouses to talk and listen to each other for the benefit of their relationship.

CHAPTER 9

Don't Dissolve It, but Resolve It

Finally, brethren, whatsoever things are true, whatsoever things are honest, whatsoever things are just, whatsoever things are pure, whatsoever things are lovely, whatsoever things are of good report; if there be any virtue, and if there be any praise, think on these things. –King James Bible,
1769/2017, Philippians 4:8

Every time the Devil tempts you to doubt the suitability of your spouse, recall the advice of Apostle Paul in the above epigraph. In most cases, a lot of the spouses fail to notice its importance until their marriage is over and done with. Instead of taking our marriage for granted, we should be capable of realizing its importance before the "water has been spilled." We need to stand up and fight for our marriage to work. For the sake of the children and your mental as well as physical health, nurture your marriage. As we have learned before, God created the first bond between man and woman in the Garden of Eden through Adam and Eve. By doing so, he sanctified marriage as an institution that needs to be protected no matter how difficult it might be.

Fight for Your Marriage

One of the most painful things in a marriage is failing to recognize its importance until it's too late, and it can't be saved (Gottman, 2002). You don't want a divorce, yet you're not sure how to avoid one. What you view as a challenge, modern society makes it seem easy, namely, for you to lift up your hands in surrender and move on. Sometimes your resolve is tested by the way people talk about marriage, regularly making you doubt its worthiness. Your friends might even remind you that marriage is simply a piece of paper that you can destroy and walk away from. Before you go ahead and quit, have you ever imagined just how simple it is for someone to tell you to do something that you have not taken time to ponder over? Be careful and safeguard your marriage from third parties who are intent on causing divorce. Gottman also says, "Only when all papers are signed, the household property split, and ex-spouses move into separate rented apartments, does the realization of just how much they have lost by giving up on their marriage kick in." What I can tell you my brothers and sisters, is that if you make the choice to fight for that marriage of yours, God will help you win the war against divorce. Frequently, a great marriage is not given the merit, nurturing, and respect it deserves until it is too late (Gottman, 2002). Let us ask God to help us fight for our marriages and not easily give up on them. The Bible describes God as our leader, our bulletproof vest, our castle, and the pillar of our power. In Psalm 33:18 the Bible reminds us that "The eyes of God are placed on the people who fear and respect him and on the people who have hope in his unfailing power and love" (*KJB*, 1769/2017).

God Wants Your Marriage to Work

In Genesis 2:23, Adam refers to his wife as "bone of bones and meat of my meat" that God, the Creator united as one. Fast forward to the time of the Messiah, thousands of years later, when Jesus tells His worshipers that marriage is a covenant that is much more than a contract with God. Recall that in the beginning, when God created man and woman, He said, "Because of this reason man will walk out of his father's house and live with his wife, bonding the two in one flesh. This means that they become one flesh and no longer two" (*KJB*, 1769/2017). According to Matthew 19:5-6, "Man must not separate what God has brought together" (*KJB*, 1769/2017). Marriage is a contractual agreement made by one man with one woman in the presence of God, with the goal of living and loving each other until death does them apart. According to Ephesians 5:22-33, the agreement that is made in marriage was crafted to reflect the tight covenant between Jesus and his worshipers (*KJB*, 1769/2017). So, after reading this section, you will be in a position to understand exactly why battling for your marriage is important to God. Each moment that we spend seeking to sort out the conflict in our marriages, we are implicitly reaffirming our commitment to Jesus.

How to Fight for Your Marriage

Never Surrender Your Marriage

All marriages go through challenges. Those difficulties are supposed to strengthen our love for our significant other, being intended to strengthen our bond with God. When the challenges become unbearable, it's good to seek help. Consider consulting a marriage counselor or watching Youtube videos for married couples. The list of things to do is endless. All strong marriages take some dedication as well as good communication between the spouses.

Protect Your Marriage.

God always draws us to his side, and according to Revelation 21:4, "One day, Jesus will come back to Earth to end all wrong doing" (*KJB*, 1769/2017). Satan, in the meantime, will never rest as he will go all-out to destroy us. His actions can include encouraging divorces, with the goal of rendering Christians ineffective. Although marriages have been created by God, they are at the mercy of the devil. The bible declares in John 10:10 that "The thief cometh not, but for to steal, and to kill, and to destroy: I am come that they might have life, and that they might have [it] more abundantly" (KJB,1769/2017). The Devil is the thief who comes to steal, to kill and destroy everything that belongs to us including our marriages. The good news is that there is an abundance of life available for us through the grace of the Lord Jesus Christ.

Pray for Your Marriage

The ultimate path to the survival of your marriage is determined by the amount of prayers you undertake. Satan can't overcome the onslaught brought upon him by prayer. Prayer brings your requirements in line with the will of God, so each time you pray for your marriage, request God Almighty to intervene and help you to love your spouse through His eyes. Also plead with Him to give you the power to sort out the mess in your marriage. Romans 12:9-12 speaks volumes when it says, "Let God change you, while believing Him to also transform your spouse" (*KJB*, 1769/2017). This teaches us to accept the actions of God when he seeks to transform our marriages from bad to the best.

The Impact of Divorce on the Family

Divorce Affects Children

Just like marital conflict, divorce brings challenges for the family. Parents need to adjust to new court orders on parenting issues, while the children will be learning new ways of being parented. Effects of divorce on the children vary from case to case. Some children accept divorce and its consequences, while other children might suffer from the transition. Let's now look at some general effects of divorce on children:

- **They struggle academically:** Divorce is challenging for everyone in the household. Such difficulties can make the academic life of the children extremely hard. They can lose interest, become withdrawn, disturbed, and confused. The greater the disruption, the higher their chances of failing in their school work.

- **They stop socializing:** The children of a broken marriage can withdraw from any forms of social activity, usually due to fear of being ridiculed by their peers. They find it difficult to relate to other people, often choosing to lead a reclusive life with few social contacts.

- **They have trouble adjusting to post-divorce life:** When divorce occurs, the children become subjected to rapid changes in the routines and rules governing their lives. They have too much information to absorb in such a short period of time, forcing them to go into overdrive and breakdown. Think of things such as new family politics, new home or living arrangement, schools, buddies, and much more. Adjusting to the new things in their lives might just become too much of a burden, leading to depression, burnout, and anxiety.

- **They develop anger issues:** In most divorce cases, where the children are overburdened and fail to receive proper counseling, they may become agitated and highly irritated. Their anger might be aimed at their parents, but they might also be blaming themselves and their friends for the divorce.

Effects on the Couples

Emotional consequences of divorce on ex-spouses might vary from moderate to severe. For ex-spouses, they might experience some or all of the symptoms mentioned below:

- Feelings of loneliness and social cut-off.
- Reduced productivity at work.
- Anxiety, burnout, and depression.
- Reduced self-esteem.
- Increased substance abuse.
- Loss of identity especially the women when they had previously used the man's name.

Effects on In-laws, Siblings, and Friends

The following are consequences of divorce on the lives of siblings, in-laws, and friends:

- They are most likely to also get divorced in their marriages.
- Friendships between couples may dissolve.
- Group outings and events might never be the same again.
- Maintaining neutrality might be challenging

As we draw this chapter to a conclusion, we want to go back to the bible text that we opened with in Philippians 4:9 which declares "Those things, which ye have both learned, and received, and heard, and seen in me, do: and the God of peace shall be with you(KJB, 1769/2017) .

What Apostle Paul is teaching us in the above text is that, we should put into practice everything that we are learning from him as he has received from the Lord. By doing everything up to our sleeves not to dissolve our marriages but rather resolve them and we shall receive the perfect peace (shalom) of God.

Questionnaire and Exercises

Questionnaire

- Who or what is responsible for the crisis in your marriage?

- Do you think your marriage can improve?

- Do you have any issues outside your marriage that are causing your unhappiness?

- Are you aware that the divorce rate is high? What can you do to make sure our marriage is not part of the divorce statistics?

- What do the Scriptures teach us about marriage and divorce?

Exercises

Bucket List Exercise

Happy couples are kind to each other. Expose yourself as a couple to new things as a relationship-building activity. Start by writing a bucket list of items you would love to do as a couple. Include both the short and long term goals in order to make it more worthwhile. Make sure that the activity you select is covered by the metrics below:

- You and your spouse can do it together

- Something that you can do regularly

- Something you can both enjoy
- Encourages productive communication

Try to undertake at least one activity every month.

CHAPTER 10

There Is Still Hope for Your Future

For there is hope of a tree, if it be cut down, that it will sprout again, and that the tender branch thereof will not cease.-King James Bible,
1769/2017, Job 14:7

The Bible, through Job 14:7, teaches us that we must have hope for the future of our marriages (*KJB*, 1769/2017). No matter how much conflict we have been exposed to, we must still seek the divine help of the living God in order to make our marriages last. This is why we can equate our marriages to the life of a tree. When it is cut, it sprouts again and it "lives to see another day." The purpose of this chapter is to assure the couples that in spite of all the challenges their marriage is facing or has been through, there is still hope for the future of their relationship. The past years have subjected your marriage to all types of things: the good, the bad, and the ugly. Because of all the things that have taken place, the marriage might seem like it's over, done, and dusted; however, every marriage has its ups and downs. All marriages or relationships face their own storms and rough patches, but, in the name of the Lord Jesus Christ our savior, I want to assure you that all hope is not lost. The time for peace and success in your marriage has arrived. You have turned the corner, and hope is all you need right now.

Hope Keeps Us Focused

All great things come to those who wait! The same expression can be made about having hope for your marriage. In hope, we find change, maturity, and spiritual growth. Here's what happens with waiting: While it might cause a lot of anxiety, it can also positively assist you to develop extreme strength that develops gradually over time. It might be difficult to notice the results in the short-term because the strength might build up slowly, but reality is that it's indeed growing inside you. You might think that all the efforts you invested in waiting have been wasted, but when your marriage is saved, you will realize that it was worth waiting for. The truth is, there is no way of really knowing how different things would be if you were somehow able to go back and fix or undo something, or change someone's mind, but no matter how idyllic your vision of what could have been, there is so much growth that happens when you can let it go, and embrace the reality that here, in the now, there is still a life worth living for. There is still hope for the future. And the more you are able to do this, the more you will grow in strength, even while you are waiting.

And remember that the ability to maintain hope will vary from individual to individual. There could be another person in your life who is willing to wait for the revival of their marriage, and you notice her strength. You admire the manner in which they gracefully keep the peace in their marriage and how courageous they deal with their deepest fears and still manage to maintain a smile on their face. So, what is different about you? No matter what you're going through right now, there is hope. If you are waiting for an outcome, you are just the same as that person you know who is patient and has hope. If you struggle to understand yourself and fail to produce that smile today, it's all fine. It does not imply that you are weak. As a couple fighting to save their marriage, it is worthwhile to remain hopeful even when things don't work out. Yes, time has lapsed while you have been trying to resolve the conflict in your marriage, and you can't recover it, but now, all the things that happened have enlightened you: your marriage is worth every penny and more than that. With hope, you can see that even though waiting for your marriage to recover might be one of the most difficult things you might have ever done; now you can concentrate on the path to recovery. Hope allows you to pause for a moment and reflect as you take deep breaths with the knowledge that just by being where you are right now, the story of your marriage isn't over yet and is about to change Let us look at some of elements that can bring hope to our seemingly dead marriages.

- *Marriage Counseling Gives Hope*

The conflict in your marriage or relationship has been going on for some time now, but through marriage counseling, you have managed to weather the storm. You were able to undergo therapy and guidance that made you realize that there is an opportunity to save your marriage. The dark and stormy days might have left your marriage in danger of collapse, but the marriage counselor has given you hope and trust that you will work together as a couple to save the marriage that you worked so hard to establish. The sun will rise again in the morning, while the moon will shine once more in the dark night sky. Turn to God, and your marriage will be saved. The Heavenly Father, in Luke 11: 9-13 says, "Ask and you will receive, knock and the door shall be opened, and seek and you will find, for the love of the Lord has no end" (*KJB*, 1769/2017). In this teaching, what our Father in Heaven is simply saying to you and me is that no matter what challenges we are facing, there is still hope and salvation through His help. God gives us hope that we will recover from the marital problems that we face, and we will be able to live with the spouses that we desire. There is no reason why our marriages should collapse, for the great God is walking with us. Marriage counseling makes you see that love has no bounds, and there is so much room for saving your marriage. Hope is the weapon that the marriage counselor will give you to begin recovering the pieces of your marriage.

- *Jesus Is Hope*

Colossians 1:27 says, "Christ is our Hope for victory" (*KJB*, 1769/2017). If taken in the context of our marriages, this verse means that we can look upon Jesus Christ, the Messiah, as the beacon of hope for the success of our marriages and relationships. Jesus Christ is the way forward, and we must ensure that we seek his love and help when we want to save our marriages. The Holy Bible teaches us that Jesus Christ is a powerful source of hope. Hebrews 12:2 refers to Jesus as "the provider of our hope; who endured the cross, despising the shame, to sit at the right hand of the throne of God" (*KJB*, 1769/2017). Again, we can have hope and peace of mind in the fact that in Matthew 6:22, Jesus says to us, "The light of the body is the eye: if therefore thine eye be single, thy whole body shall be full of light" (KJB, 1769/2017). The figurative meaning of "eye" in the bible is "concentration and focus," implying that looking up to a single source, Lord Jesus is the only way to maintain hope and trust that our marriages will be saved. There is a certain part of us that is ignited by sight. Hebrews 12:2 encourages us to focus our eyes on Jesus for He gave us the example (*KJB*, 1769/2017). Jesus focused His eyes on the happiness that was in front of Him, and avoided concentrating on the cross He was about to carry. He avoided being shameful by not focusing on the pain he was subjected to. The big lesson is that we must begin to absorb the pressures of conflict in our marriages by looking away from any marital problems that we are facing and looking unto Jesus instead. Keep your eyes and mind on Him and don't forget his words.

- *Good Company gives Hope*

As we have discussed before that "Bad company corrupt good morals" (1 Corinthians 15:33 KJB, 1769/2017) in relation to whom do you run to for an advice in your marriage? On the contrary, a good company will enrich your morals and hence your marriage or relationship. The two of you can befriend a God-fearing couple who are older than you in marriage or even on the same level as you, for accountability, as checks and balances and encouragement to each other.

"For as iron sharpeneth iron so a man sharpeneth the countenance of his friend". Proverbs 27:17 KJB, 1769/2017)

How to Maintain Hope as a Christian

In Jeremiah 31:3, we read that "The Lord came upon us in the past, and said: I loved you eternally; I have protected you with total commitment" (*KJB*, 1769/2017). This verse is a reminder that God provides eternal hope for us. He will not forsake us, but will do everything possible to protect our marriages. As Christians, we need to have hope and live in Christ. I recommend some of the following tactics to manage and maintain hope in your marriage, the Christian way.

Meditate

One definite method of having hope and trust in Jesus Christ is to practice mindfulness on His Word. As we wake up in the morning, we should start to meditate using his powerful Word, and this focus should be followed throughout the entire day. In the words of Joshua in verse 1:8, "Meditating through the word of God can attract success and victory" (*KJB*, 1769/2017). Joshua teaches us that when we pray to God and practice mindfulness, we can bring success and eliminate conflict in our marriages. We must always think about the kindness of Jesus as we meditate, focusing on how he can help our marriages to survive. In our minds, we must play out the scenes when Jesus performed miracles in the Bible because they provide proof that He has the power to help us with our problems. These can include the following:

- The raising of the widow's son in Luke 7:11-17 (*KJB*, 1769/2017).

- Feeding of the 5000 in Mark 6:30-44 (*KJB*, 1769/2017).
- Healing of a paralyzed man in Luke 5:18-19 (*KJB*, 1769/2017).
- The raising of Lazarus from the dead in John 11:38-44 (*KJB*, 1769/2017).

All the points stated above are a great indication that our seemingly dead marriages can rise up again, if we meditate in the name of the Living God.

Supplicate

We must kneel down as a couple to seek help from our Lord. When we pray together as a couple, we will enhance the bond between us and God. It gets stronger with each prayer that we make, and we will always have hope that our prayers will be answered. We must focus on prayers in order to avoid the pressures and challenges of conflict in marital life.

Action Speaks Louder Than Words!

Let's take time to put our prayers into action. What I mean is that instead of simply praying and asking God to stop the conflict in our marriages, we must start taking the necessary steps to physically avoid marital conflict. We can explore things such as counseling, going out on date nights, watching TV together as a couple, and cooking together. We must make the effort to convert our prayers into action. Remember that God helps those who work towards helping themselves!

Victory against Divorce Is Guaranteed in the Eyes of God

In Joel 2:25, God says, "And I will give you back the years consumed by the locust and the army of worms that I sent among you" (*KJB*, 1769/2017). We are encouraged to teach us to look up to God's salvation for victory in our marriages. God will restore all the things that you might have lost through the conflict in your marriage. If you have lost faith and trust in your spouse, God has the power to give it back to you. If you suffered injuries from the abuse perpetrated by your spouse, the Heavenly Father can heal those wounds and help you to fully recover. With God, victory is certain! Divorce is an enemy of marriage, and we need to seek divine intervention in order to defeat it. Let us be like King David who clearly understood the presence of God in his life. By reading and correctly interpreting the verses in the psalms, we will understand the reason why it was personally and emotionally important for him to remember that God was always with him.

I remember the preaching in 2 Samuel 8, on how King David wanted to build a house for God (*KJB*, 1769/2017). Significantly, because David and his kingdom were going through a period of peace and tranquillity, the king offered to build a house in God's honor, to thank Him for the good times that they were enjoying. By the way, this is the house that was supposed to permanently keep the Ark of the Covenant. God, however, told David that He himself was going to construct a house for him as an eternal legacy for David, through whose lineage the Messiah would arrive! A few years later, David's nation is attacked, but God gives them victory by destroying their enemies.

What lesson does this episode teach us? How can we relate David's experience with God to the stories of our own marriages? Because of his unwavering commitment and belief that God deserved to be rewarded and worshiped, the Heavenly Father preserved David's life against all adversities that he came across. God guided David, keeping him safe and giving him hope, ultimately ensuring the victory that he needed against his enemies. King David was a military tactician–recall how he killed Goliath; however, in this case, his victories were not due to his military might or his leadership abilities. David was not following any principles of war like all generals do, but his victory came from the faith God had in him. He was blessed and protected by God. Don't we all want to receive this blessing and protection from God? I certainly do!

Just like King David, we can receive this protection in our marriages too. The enemy of a happy marriage is conflict, which leads to divorce if left unresolved. We must have faith that we too can store the Ten Commandments within our bodies. This will be similar to David offering to build a home for the Ark of the Covenant. As soon as we embody the Ten Commandments or the Living Word of God, we become better people who are able to manage some of the causes of conflict in our marriages. For instance, "thou shall not commit adultery" is a commandment that prevents fornication and thus keeps our marriages safe. There are two commandments–"thou shalt not kill" and "thou shall not steal"–that if broken, can land you in jail and thus jeopardize your marriage. By observing these commandments, you can save your marriage and become victorious against divorce.

Questionnaire and Exercises

Questionnaire

- How are we going to fix the damage caused by conflict to our marriage?

- In your opinion, what can we do as a couple to strengthen our marriage?

- What aspect of your life can you give up in order to avoid a divorce?

- How will remaining committed to this marriage save our marriage?

- What do we gain by continuing this conflict?

Exercises

Selective Argument Exercise

Picking your fights is as important as managing them. You need to know how to select and manage your conflicts. What counts is not just making statements, but the action taken to fulfill those statements. Delaying something for a couple of days allows you to gain perspective in the process and evaluate if the argument is really necessary. The good thing is that such actions enable you to enter the conversation in a relaxed manner and with proper arguments. Each time you get into a dispute that you don't seem to agree with, conduct the following exercise as a couple:

Any major disputes that you can't avoid should not be postponed. They should be addressed by all means necessary, so this exercise is not an excuse to assist you to sweep problems under the carpet. The rule is that anything that can't be remembered by Sunday was definitely not a high priority. This exercise is critical for couples because it gives them the benefit of learning how to give priority to certain conflicts as time passes.

Conclusion

Be ye angry, and sin not: let not the sun go down upon your wrath. –King James Bible,
1769/2017, Ephesians 4:26

The verse in the epigraph above teaches us that we must remain in total control of ourselves, even when we are angry, and avoid sinning. Instead, as we have emphasized throughout this book, we must learn to love one another in the name of God, and marriage provides the perfect opportunity to do so. For any marriage to work, the love must be unconditional, which will ensure that the spouses meet each other's needs and solve problems as a team. In turn, team work depends on great communication to be effective; if a spouse is not a good communicator, the relationship will suffer.

At the same time, however, conflict avoidance is not only unhealthy for marriage, but also impossible. If you think that all satisfied couples lead a life devoid of marital conflict, think again. Bear in mind that, as shown in this book, each time two different people come together, there is bound to be different opinions and ideologies. In a marriage, one spouse can't duplicate the traits of the other spouse, and this is what makes a marriage unique. Whenever we experience conflict in our marriages, we have to move in swiftly to resolve the conflict before it escalates into a "war" that can lead to divorce. The negative effects of conflict on marriage are numerous, but we can sum them up as follows: deteriorating health, burnout, depression, heart disease, and eating disorders.

The good thing is that conflict resolution and good marriage communication are skills that we can cultivate and practice in the name of God our Creator, who is prepared to guide us through any marital challenges that we might experience. We need to deploy problem-solving strategies that can minimize the threat of marital conflicts in order for us to foster a healthy relationship with our spouses. Marital conflicts also negatively impact our children. Basically, such relationship conflicts pile negative pressure and energy on our children, so much so that the children feel insecure and victimized. Conflict in relationships is triggered by some of the following factors:

- Incompatible beliefs, goals, and needs.
- Bad communication skills.
- Excessive emotional responses.

During periods of conflict in your marital relationship, you might lose touch with your emotions or feel stressed by the actions of your spouse. In such cases, avoid freaking out or withdrawing into yourself to avoid conflict, but make attempts to resolve it amicably and reasonably. Matthew 7:12, says, "So in all things, do unto others as you want them to do to you, according to the Law and the Prophets" (KJB, 1769/2017). Matthew teaches us to love one another and to ensure that every action we take against another person must be fair and acceptable to us. Don't demand that your spouse tend to the garden every weekend, yet you never even spend one day in the same garden.

Both spouses need to decide how they intend to compromise on several matters while remaining true to themselves. Thus, they might establish solutions that accommodate each spouse's preferences or a way for both of them to remain committed to resolving the conflict.

In marriages, small matters are easy to resolve, so you should not dwell on them as they waste your time. For example, disagreements over what to cook for Sunday lunch, or conflict over how to squeeze toothpaste from the tube should be easily handled without any third parties involved. It is those bigger issues that involve people's emotions, faith, trust, and values, that require you to establish solutions that prevent a total breakdown of the marriage. For instance, if your spouse cheats on you, and you can prove it to be true, then you will need to resort to counseling and relationship-building exercises in order to make the marriage work.

No one deserves more attention than your spouse. You need to be able to adequately manage the influence of in-laws as these folks can make or break a marriage if you fail to set boundaries for them. They should know their place in your life. Let them know when they can visit your home as well as when to stop interfering in your life. Couples should make sure that they stay in touch with each other throughout the day. Always text, chat, or call each other. Your spouse should be the main contact person in your life. Be your spouse's best friend, and your marriage will work out for the better.

Effective communication skills, both verbal and nonverbal, are essential elements for the health of a marriage because relationships involve emotions. When you communicate with your spouse, you need to be kind, understanding, and respectful because this is the only way to show them true love. You should also be able to read their body language because this will help you see how they react in an argument. Remember that not all of us are good verbal communicators, so body language is an important tool that you can use to your advantage, one that can ultimately benefit your marriage! In instances of parenting and co-parenting, communication is way more important than anything else because parents are involved in grooming children who will one day be parents. Children learn how to effectively communicate by seeing and hearing their parents or guardians speak. Finally, as the worst enemy of your marriage, bad communication is the main reason behind the rise in the number of divorce cases globally.

Whatever the nature of our conflicts, we must always remember that divorce is not an option. When God brought Adam and Eve together in the Garden of Eden as man and wife, this was the beginning of the act known as "marriage." It is God who sanctioned this first marriage, so we should all respect Him for doing so. In fact we need to honor Him for his act of love, and the only way for us to do this is by making sure that our marriages work. Hope is what God has given us as a weapon to fight conflict in our marriages and ultimately avoid divorce. We can keep hope alive in our marriages by praying for each other and requesting for God's power to prevail in keeping our marriages intact. According to the words of Pastor Matthew Ashimolowo, "It has not ended until you are victorious, it has not ended until you defeat the enemy, it has not ended until the Heavenly Father tells you it has ended." With his teaching, The Man of God is simply giving us strength to compel us to remain hopeful and determined to overcome all the adversities facing our marriages and relationships. We must not give up, but always look towards finding resolutions to our marital and relationship problems through the divine grace of God.

Now that you have all the tools, go out there and use them, and remember that there is still hope for the future of your marriage. All the problems that your marriage is currently facing, or faced in the past, can be overcome. God is the only way to a successful marriage!

Thank you for reading this book! If you enjoyed it and found very helpful, I would be extremely grateful if you could take a few minutes to leave a review on Amazon. Your honest, positive and constructive feedback will not only help others, but will help me continue to improve, mature and grow as an author.

References

Ashimolowo, M. (1997). *It's not over 'til it's over.* Destiny Image Pub.

Baumgardner, J. (2020, July 8). *Help! My in-laws are ruining my marriage!* First Things First. https://firstthings.org/help-my-in-laws-are-ruining-my-marriage/

Beaty, J. (2017, February 13). *4 negative behaviors that may be making you sick.* The Gottman Institute. https://www.gottman.com/blog/4-negative-behaviors-may-making-sick

Bonnie. (2020, August 19). *Relationships: The 4 styles of communication - relationships: The 4 styles of communication %.* https://www.skinnerpsychotherapy.com/relationships-the-4-styles-of-communication/#:~:text=There%20are%20a%20number%20of

Brown, J. (2021, November 19). *5 ways to build a better friendship with your husband.* Jehava Brown Blog. https://jehavabrownblog.com/better-friendship-with-your-husband/

Cearlock. (2021, October 31). *Types of marital conflict*. The Mindly Group, PLLC. https://themindlygroup.com/types-of-marital-conflict/#:~:text=There%20are%20two%20%20types%20of

Feuerman, M. (2022, September 20). *How much sex is enough in a marriage or relationship?* Verywell Mind. https://www.verywellmind.com/how-much-sex-do-we-need-4057000

Gottman, J. (2002). *The seven principles for making marriage work*. Harmony.

Gurevich. (2018). *8 causes of infertility-related relationship tension and ways to cope*. Verywell Family. https://www.verywellfamily.com/how-infertility-impact-your-marriage-and-relationship-4121098

King James Bible. (2017). *King James Bible Online.* https://www.kingjamesbibleonline.org/ (Original work published 1769)

Leath, A. (2020, March 25). *30 bible verses about the beauty of marriage*. Country Living. https://www.countryliving.com/life/g31913092/bible-verses-about-marriage/

Love Is Respect. (2020). *Conflict resolution*. Love Is Respect. https://www.loveisrespect.org/resources/conflict-resolution/

McCoy, K. P., George, M. R. W., Cummings, E. M., & Davies, P. T. (2013). *Constructive and destructive marital conflict, parenting, and children's school and social adjustment*. Social Development, n/a-n/a. https://doi.org/10.1111/sode.12015

Merriam-Webster. (2022). *Merriam-webster dictionary*. Merriam-Webster.com; Merriam-Webster. https://www.merriam-webster.com/

Meyer. (2017). *10 marital problems that cause divorce*. LiveAbout. https://www.liveabout.com/marital-problems-that-cause-divorce-1102945

Meyer, C. (2022, September 22). *5 different types of infidelity*. Brides. https://www.brides.com/different-types-of-infidelity-1102872#:~:text=Infidelity%2C%20%20or%20%20cheating%2C%20is%20the

Nguyen, J. (2020, May 19). *Why everyone's talking about love languages these days & how to find yours*. Mindbodygreen. https://www.mindbodygreen.com/articles/the-5-love-languages-explained

Onu, D. (2022, November 4). *4 important physical needs in marriage to know - David Onu*. Davidonu.com. https://davidonu.com/physical-needs-in-marriage/

Peale, N. V. (2022). *The power of positive thinking*: Amazon.co.uk: Peale, Norman Vincent: 9789355994226: Books. Amazon.co.uk. https://www.amazon.co.uk/Power-Positive-Thinking-Norman-%20Vincent/dp/9355994222/ref=sr_1_3?crid=P0EHSJQ6H7AY&keywords=the+power+of+positive+thinking+norman+vincent+peale&qid=1668094064&s=books&sprefix=the+power+of+positive+thinking%2Cstripbooks%2C298&sr=1-3

Rosberg, G., & Rosberg, B. (2006). *Building spiritual intimacy in your marriage*. Focus on the Family.

https://www.focusonthefamily.ca/content/building-spiritual-intimacy-in-your-marriage

Rush, B. (2020, October 29). *5 types of communication in marriage: why they're essential to a healthy relationship - Body+Mind Magazine*. Bodymind.com. https://bodymind.com/5-types-of-communication-in-marriage-why-theyre-essential-to-a-healthy-relationship/

Sara Stillman Berger. (2019, June 28). *The secret to having a happy marriage*. Oprah Daily; Oprah Daily. https://www.oprahdaily.com/life/relationships-love/a28186035/how-to-have-a-happy-marriage/

Schnell, S. L. (2016, September 10). *The importance of friendship in marriage*. Psych Central. https://psychcentral.com/blog/the-importance-of-friendship-in-marriage#1

Temple, M. (2009). *Ten secrets to a successful marriage - focus on the family*. Focus on the Family. https://www.focusonthefamily.com/marriage/ten-secrets-to-a-successful-marriage/

University of Rochester Medical Center. (2019). *The keys to a successful marriage - health encyclopedia - university of rochester medical center*. Rochester.edu. https://www.urmc.rochester.edu/encyclopedia/content.aspx?contenttypeid=1&contentid=4580

www.ingramcontent.com/pod-product-compliance
Lightning Source LLC
Chambersburg PA
CBHW030304100526
44590CB00012B/513